Learn to Play
Good Cricket

Learn to Play
Good Cricket

Mohinder Amarnath

UBSPD

UBS Publishers' Distributors Ltd.

New Delhi • Mumbai • Bangalore • Madras •
Calcutta • Patna • Kanpur • London

UBS Publishers' Distributors Ltd.

5 Ansari Road, New Delhi-110 002
Phones : 3273601, 3266646 ☆ *Cable* : ALLBOOKS ☆ *Fax* : (91) 11-327-6593
e-mail: ubspd.del@smy.sprintrpg.ems.vsnl.net.in
Internet; www.ubspd.com
Apeejay Chambers, 5 Wallace Street, Mumbai-400 001
Phones : 2076971, 2077700 ☆ *Cable* : UBSIPUB ☆ *Fax* : 2070827
10 First Main Road, Gandhi Nagar, Bangalore-560 009
Phones : 2263901, 2263902, 2253903 ☆ *Cable* : ALLBOOKS ☆ *Fax* : 2263904
6, Sivaganga Road, Nungambakkam, Chennai-600 034
Phone : 8276355, 8270189 ☆ *Cable* : UBSIPUB ☆ *Fax* : 8278920
8/1-B, Chowringhee Lane, Calcutta-700 016
Phones : 2441821, 2442910, 2449473 ☆ *Cable* : UBSIPUBS ☆ *Fax* : 2450027
5 A, Rajendra Nagar, Patna-800 016
Phones : 672856, 656170 ☆ *Cable* : UBSPUB ☆ *Fax* : 656169
80, Noronha Road, Cantonment, Kanpur-208 004
Phones : 369124, 362665, 357488 ☆ *Fax* : 315122

© Mohinder Amarnath

First Published	1996
First Reprint	1997
Second Reprint	1997
Third Reprint	1997
Fourth Reprint	1998
Fifth Reprint	1998

Cover Design : UBS Art Studio.

Designed & Typeset in 11pt. Baskerville at Alphabets, New Delhi
Printed at Nutech Photolithographers Shahdara, Delhi

To
All young cricketers who love
the game and want to learn
its finer points

Foreword

Sunil Gavaskar

I am happy to know that Mohinder Amarnath is writing a book on the basics of playing cricket. Mohinder or 'Jimmy', as he has been popularly called, has not only been India's foremost player but has also been known to be a deep thinker on the intricacies of the game.

Starting his career for India as a new ball bowler who could bat, he went on to become one of India's most reliable batsmen in tests and in the limited overs version, its key player with both bat and ball. Unfortunately for Mohinder, when he started his career in 1969-70, all-rounders were not in fashion and by all-rounder one means a player who could be in the side on the strength of his batting or his bowling. There were plenty of bits-and-pieces players and Mohinder got slotted into that. It was only in 1976 when he got the opportunity to bat at number three that Mohinder's career started to blossom. Still, with the middle order competition for places being as strong as ever he was in and out of the side frequently.

Being a serious thoughtful cricketer he did not take these omissions as a joke but continued to work harder. Mohinder's career is a glittering example of what hard work can do. Along with the intense physical conditioning also went the mental preparation. So, when he got back in the team once again in 1982 it was with a wide open, two-eyed stance. This enabled him to cope with the extra pace of Imran Khan and the West Indies quartet in such a spectacular fashion that he scored over 1100 runs in 11 tests against Pakistan and the West Indies. He reverted to the side-on orthodox stance the following season. It is just this ability to adapt, while keeping to the basics, that separates the great players from the good ones.

Technique is vital to a player for without the proper technique one cannot survive at the top level. What is equally important is temperament which is really within a person.

It would be tremendous for the youngsters hoping to make a mark in the game to learn from what Mohinder says about technique and it would do them a world of good if they could pick up from him the way he strengthened himself mentally to counter everything that was thrown at him on and off the field.

There is no better example to follow than Mohinder Amarnath's on how to become a self-made cricketer.

Preface

Mohinder Amarnath

The basic purpose of writing this book is to provide fundamental guidelines to aspiring youngsters to develop their game properly and systematically and emerge as complete cricketers. Others will also find the contents useful as a reference source in order to improve upon their game or to learn more about its myriad facets.

Over the years, the game of cricket has, inevitably, undergone several changes, especially after the advent of the thrilling one-day matches. Consequently, I have tried to bring the subject matter as up to date as possible.

I would like to express my everlasting gratitude to my father, Shri Lala Amarnath, who has several noteworthy achievements to his credit in the cricketing world. Whatever I have accomplished, I attribute to his inspiring guidance and practical advice. I recall how my father would take us (my two brothers, Surinder and Rajinder, and myself) to the maidan and give us proper (and regular) coaching in all departments of cricket. He ensured that we learnt the various aspects of the game sincerely and purposefully. He constantly stressed the importance of self-discipline, regular practice, hard work and dedication as also the will to perform to the best of one's ability, be it a practice session or a match. He spent long hours not only explaining the intricacies of various techniques but also demonstrating how to use them practically. He would watch us in action and later point out our strengths and weaknesses and how to develop the former and get rid of the latter. He always encouraged us to play our natural game.

My father was the one who helped me overcome the faults in my technique, especially when I underwent a bad patch against the West Indies. He used to remind me often that cricket is a gentleman's game and should be played strictly according to the rules.

I sincerely hope that this book will prove useful to all my readers in learning the basics and also the finer points of the game. I wish all success to my young readers who, through perseverance and determination, could emerge as future Sunil Gavaskars, Kapil Devs or Sachin Tendulkars.

Contents

One

My Cricketing Pitch:
What Cricket Means to Me

When I was asked to write this book, I thought it would be a relatively simple job. All I had to do was draw upon my fairly long cricketing experience and spice up the narrative with a few pithy and enthralling personal anecdotes. However, the task proved to be much more formidable than I had imagined, mainly because cricket is not merely a game but much more than that. For me, cricket represents a positive frame of mind; a lifestyle; and above all, an inspiring and delightful experience. Thus, I am writing this book to share with everyone my experiences at the national and international levels, including the nuggets of knowledge and wisdom that I picked up from my father Shri Lala Amarnath, a renowned and respected cricketer. I would also like to recount the hard toil and sweat-filled days at the nets and then on the field. I remember playing cricket, as a kid, on the streets and parks. My ambition was to move forward in life; to achieve something substantial and to establish an identity of my own.

Through this book, I am trying to give something back to the game. I have come across a lot of talented children playing cricket on the roads and parks, but many of them face a bleak future as they cannot afford the proper equipment and the guidance of a professional coach. I am writing this book, hoping it will prove beneficial to such children.

This book is devoted to the game of cricket as a whole, and is not restricted to batting or bowling or fielding. Since I strongly believe that the time-tested, old methods are still worthwhile and useful, I have adopted the traditional patterns. However, this does not imply that I am opposed to improvisation or the introduction of new techniques as and when required. What I would like to stress is that the foundation should be firm and solid and the structural design can be modified to suit each individual's capability and temperament.

In cricket, winning is important or at least playing to win is, as Sunil Gavaskar asserted on my TV programme. He also maintained that the game is not finished until the last ball has been bowled.

1

Cricket is a game for all kinds of people. A youngster need not be born with the physical make-up of an athlete to play well nor does he or she need to be an academic to appreciate its subtleties. The game captivates the young and the old, the extrovert and the introvert. Attitude and skill, both on and off the field, count very much. As K. Srikkanth puts it: "You don't have to be a first class player or test cricketer to enjoy the game. It can be played for fun and relaxation."

Cricket is also an unpredictably capricious game. It can make you laugh and cry at the same time. I thoroughly enjoyed my 1982-83 seasons in Pakistan, West Indies and England, especially during the World Cup. At that stage, I was on top of the world and had a magic touch. Nothing went wrong during that period. I was playing so well that even if I batted blindfolded I would have scored runs easily. Then came the nightmare of my cricketing life. In the next series against the West Indies at home I just could not put my bat to the ball. I scored five '0's' in six innings. While cricket can elevate one to great heights, it can also dump one in an abyss, unceremoniously. Consequently, it's always useful to remain a student of this game; that's the only way one can learn and improve. You may even learn from a club cricketer. One should be ready to learn at all times. Listen to everyone but do what you feel is correct.

In Indian cricket people praise you to the sky when you are doing well. It doesn't matter how well or how badly you are playing, as long as you are scoring runs. The moment you fail nobody wants to know you and people begin criticising you and start 'discovering' all sorts of faults in your technique and approach. The point I would like to emphasise is that such subjective judgements should not make a negative impact on any player. He should remain level headed and composed. Another unique aspect I would like to highlight is that the kind of respect and affection that a player gets from the people of India cannot be obtained anywhere else in the world.

One should not forget the wise old adage that practice makes a man perfect. Try to play the game as if you are playing in a match so that you don't make mistakes. If you can concentrate at the nets when two or more bowlers are bowling, I don't see anyone having problems concentrating during matches. This rule applies to all categories of players, i.e., bowlers, batsmen, fielders and wicket-keepers.

I can safely declare on the basis of my experience that some of the Indian test players during my playing days never concentrated while playing at the nets with the result they picked up bad habits such as being lethargic and indifferent, and paid the penalty in the matches. They then began giving the excuse of going through a bad patch. I have never believed in such rubbish because I strongly believe that whenever a batsman gets out, it is due to his own mistake. There is no unplayable delivery in my dictionary of cricket. I hate it when people think up excuses to cover their failure.

I would also like to stress the importance of the laws of cricket. Many cricketers have failed to prosper because they did not know the rules of the game properly. Many matches have been won because an enterprising captain knew the laws precisely and used that knowledge effectively. I remember playing a match in Sharjah against

Pakistan in 1989 and we were going great guns. Imran Khan, the Pakistani captain, deliberately delayed the pace and slowed down the over rate, i.e., bowling four less overs in a 50 overs game in the specified time. Pakistan scored the required runs when they batted second. I am sure if we had batted for full 50 overs, the target we would have set would have been much more stiff and may have been impossible to achieve.

I am sure several players of first class and test cricket may not be aware of *all* the rules and regulations of the game and may not even be knowing the length and width of the wicket, the crease and even the other basics of the game. They never felt the need to do so.

The main purpose behind this book is to explain the basics of the game in a simple way so that it can benefit both the beginners and the seasoned cricketers. The uniqueness of this game lies in the fact that one can enjoy it at all ages whether 10 or 50. The contents of this book are meant for right-handers. Left-handers should do the opposite. I am presuming that the readers of this book possess some fundamental knowledge of the game and the methods of playing it.

In writing this book, I have tried to ensure that the great skills that have made cricket the game it is can be appreciated by enthusiasts who want to achieve success and also simultaneously enjoy the game.

Two
Coming to 'Terms' with Cricket

Before we become too involved in analysing and understanding the various cricketing skills, it's important to understand certain concepts and terms related to the game that concern bowlers, batsmen and fielders. On acquiring this knowledge one would be able to improve one's technique on the basis of sound principles. It's important for both the batsman and the bowler to know the precise length of a delivery. For example, when a batsman picks a ball of the wrong length to hit he gets into trouble. Similarly, a bowler is hammered all over the ground if he bowls with a bad length. The only difference between good and bad players is that the good batsman identifies the precise type of delivery a few seconds earlier than other batsman. In my opinion, a good bowler is one who has control over his length.

LENGTH

What is *length* and how do you define *proper length*? The word length in cricket refers to the point at which the ball pitches in relation to the batsman in his normal stance at the wicket. You must have heard commentators and experts on radio and television, mentioning and discussing terms such as 'good length', or 'short of a length' and applying them differently to batsmen and bowlers.

A good length delivery may be described as that length of the delivery which causes the batsman the most hesitation (and discomfort) whether to play back or forward. The prime objective of every bowler is to bowl at good length at will, but many have learnt to do so only after hard toil and effort. Eminent bowlers such as Bishen Singh Bedi, Vinoo Mankad and Bapu Nadkarni could bowl precisely at one point repeatedly but they could do so only after putting in hard labour over the years. There are only few who are born with the ability to bowl at good length at will. It's difficult to define precisely a good length delivery because the concept of good length differs from person to person and depends on the individual's physical makeup. What may be a good length delivery to one person may not be so to another. Similarly, a good length delivery bowled by a pace bowler will be different in the case of a slow bowler but it provides

4

the same result, i.e., making the batsman hesitate whether to play forward or back. Weather conditions, surface and even the condition of the ball are important factors in producing a good length delivery. When a ball is new and conditions are ideal for swing bowling, the good length spot will be slightly nearer the batsman on slow wickets than it would be on hard and fast wickets.

BOUNCE

The bounce of the wicket makes a lot of difference to batsmen and bowlers. The amount of bounce depends on the nature of the playing surface. It's true that the faster the playing surface, the higher the bounce. Similarly, the slower the surface, the lower will be the bounce. Bounce also depends on the ability of the bowler. Sometimes on slow wickets, pace bowlers of the calibre of Malcolm Marshall, Imran Khan, Andy Roberts and Michael Holding could achieve amazing speed and bounce that would surprise the batsman. I remember playing against Marshall in Trinidad (in 1983) in the West Indies. Despite the fact that the wicket had slowed down on the fourth day of the test match, he had bowled a few deliveries which went past my head like missiles. I still remember a short of a length ball which whizzed in so quickly and lifted so sharply that I didn't get the time to take any defensive measures and before I knew what was happening, the ball had hit my helmet and had shot off to the boundary.

Similarly, Imran Khan produced a hostile spell in Hyderabad (Pakistan) in the 1982-83 series. He was generating amazing speed and bounce of the wicket which surprised me because other bowlers' deliveries could hardly reach the knees, whereas Imran's normal delivery would come to waist or chest height. Similarly I remember facing the Australian paceman Jeff Thomson in Perth in 1977. Wicket-keeper Steve Rixon didn't collect anything below chest height. I definitely agree that wickets make bowlers, but there is no substitute for sheer hard work and determination.

The ball bounces differently depending on whether it is new or old. A new ball is hard and has a strong seam and comes quicker on any kind of wicket and bounces more, whereas an old ball comes in slower and bounces less due to softness. The extent of bounce also depends on the height and the action of the bowler. The higher the action of the bowler, the more bounce he is bound to get. Height also plays an important role. Extremely tall bowlers, such as Curty Ambrose and Joel Garner, could generate more bounce than other bowlers. A batsman has to decide fast whether to play forward or back to a good length delivery. A good batsman always adjusts himself to the bounce of the wicket; that's how he should plan his innings as soon as he faces or watches a few deliveries. A good player always plans his batting strategy on his sighting of the ball and the bounce of the wicket. The most difficult wicket to play on is a wicket which has an unpleasant and uneven bounce. The batsman who was a master in tackling any kind of attack on such a wicket was G.R. Vishwanath. He could play with such ease as if there was nothing wrong with the surface, whereas others used to struggle throughout the game. I remember watching two of his innings: one against the West Indies at Madras in 1974-75 and the other against Australia at Melbourne in 1980-81. On both occasions, he helped India to beat the opposition. His secret was that, being a back foot player, he would gain that extra split second to time his stroke.

Good players react instinctively and always prepare themselves to tackle all kinds of difficult situations. I have played a lot of cricket with Sunil Gavaskar and the moment he found a wicket of his liking he wouldn't yield an inch. It is preferable to play more of the front foot when the bounce is low and more off the back foot when the bounce is high.

HIGH BOUNCE

What are 'high bounce' and 'low bounce'? When the ball hits the top portion of your bat, while playing on the front foot (maybe at a spot higher than the middle of your bat when playing on the back foot), it is called 'high bounce'. 'Low bounce' is said to occur when the ball hits the bat at a spot near the bottom, while playing forward or back. (See Fig.2.1.)

The more bounce a wicket offers, the attacking bowler will find it more advantageous in that he can pitch the ball closer to the batsman, thus forcing him to make mistakes. If the batsman happens to be a 'committed' player, the bowler can adjust his length accordingly. For instance, if a batsman is a committed front foot player, the observant bowler could shorten his length, and, on the other hand, if the batsman is a committed back foot player, the bowler could pitch the ball up to the former, compelling him to commit errors while playing his strokes.

A competent batsman fathoms the bowler's technique and tactics quickly, and an intelligent bowler perceives and capitalises on the weak points of a batsman very fast.

Let me now explain some common terms frequently heard on radio and television (or seen in print). (Refer to Fig.2.2.)

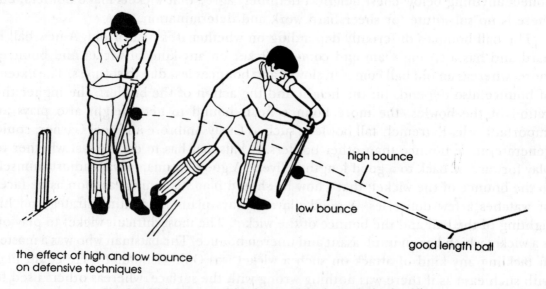

the effect of high and low bounce
on defensive techniques

Fig. 2.1 High bounce and low bounce: defensive methods of tackling

GOOD LENGTH

Every bowler strives to pitch all his deliveries on the good length spot. This spot differs from batsman to batsman. A good length delivery for a short chap may turn out to be a half volley for a tall fellow. In other words, a good length delivery is one which a batsman cannot hit and is unsure of how to play it. It is pitched at a point which is far enough from the batsman's front foot, therefore, he cannot hit it off the front foot. This delivery is always bowled up to the batsman.

LONG HOP

The very name explains this term very well. This delivery is pitched half way down the wicket. It is slow enough for a batsman to consider it a lollipop for instant hammering. It is normally hit in front of the wicket (left of the square leg umpire) by a batsman and is generally a cross-batted shot (i.e., a shot in which the ball is pulled from outside the off stump to the leg side).

SHORT BALL

A diligent bowler always tries to make a batsman play more off the front foot so as to get him out. Short bowling is effective only if the batsman is not good enough to play off the back foot and one is a fiercely quick bowler. Basically, short bowling is considered bad bowling because the ball is pitched half way down the wicket so that the batsman gets ample time to play his stroke leisurely of the back foot. Batsmen of a high standard will simply murder short bowling.

SHORT OF A LENGTH

As the name itself suggests, a short of a length delivery is one that is pitched much closer to the batsman compared to the short ball (but still short of good length). The batsman cannot normally hit such a delivery forcefully. This delivery is a useful, defensive weapon on a good wicket. It can prove very effective on uneven or bad wickets, especially when the ball tends to keep low.

HALF VOLLEY

This is the ideal delivery which every batsman should be looking forward to wallop. It is pitched beyond a good length and lands very close to the batsman's front foot, thus enabling him to hit the delivery off the front foot powerfully. However, on a seamer's wicket or where conditions are ideal for swing bowling, the half volley can provide a rich haul of victims.

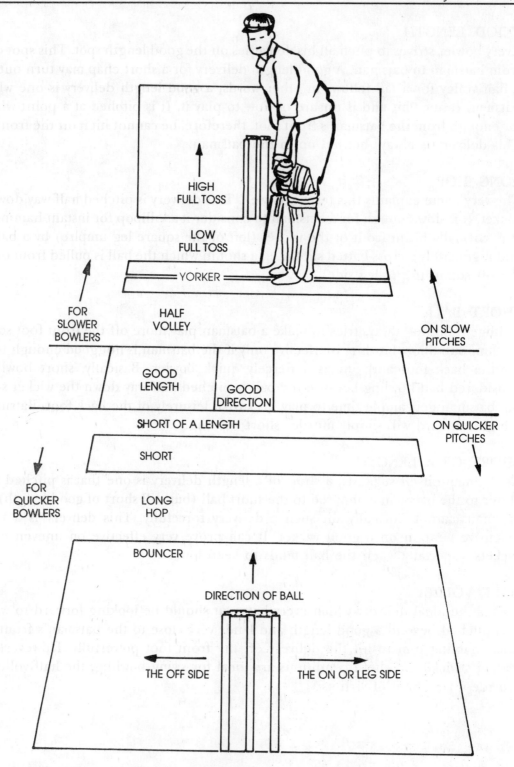

Fig.2.2 Various terms diagrammatically demarcated.

YORKER

The yorker can prove very effective in hiking a bowler's tally if delivered properly with extra pace, pitching approximately at the batsman's feet. I feel that a batsman converts a low full toss into a yorker when he plays over it. It is an ideal delivery to fox a batsman who has a high back lift, provided one can generate the requisite pace. Some very successful bowlers, who could and can produce this delivery at will, include Joel Garner, Michael Holding, Waqar Younis and Wasim Akram.

FULL TOSS

This is another 'gift' of a delivery to the batsman. As the name implies, this delivery does not pitch at all. It can be hit anywhere, depending on the height at which it reaches the batsman. It's a better delivery than a long hop because I have seen many batsmen getting out to a full toss, especially when bowled by a leg spinner. The enigmatic B.S. Chandrashekhar has captured many wickets with this delivery.

BOUNCER

This is the final and most potent weapon which a fast bowler relies on. He can either take wickets or shatter the confidence of the batsman with this particular delivery. The legitimacy of this delivery has been (and continues to be) a hotly debated topic, leading to a good deal of controversy. A 'perfect' bouncer pitches in the long hop area or within the bowler's half of the wicket; however, the extremely fast pace of delivery makes the ball lift dangerously (after pitching) towards the batsman's chest or head. In the early sixties (when helmets were not in vogue) Nari Contractor (a former Indian captain) suffered a serious head injury while facing a bouncer from West Indian paceman Charlie Griffith, which virtually ended his cricketing career. Another West Indian paceman, Andy Roberts, was a specialist in delivering bouncers and could adroitly change his pace to produce two kinds of bouncers with the same action (one of average speed and the other extremely fast), which invariably baffled the batsmen.

BEAMER

A beamer is a head-high, full toss delivery, which can sometimes prove lethal to the batsman. Consequently, a bowler should not be permitted to bowl a beamer under any circumstances.

DIRECTION

Any intelligent bowler will realise that it is very important to maintain a good length and bowl accurately. The basic aim of the bowler should be to compel the batsman to play each and every delivery. No batsman would be happy to play all six deliveries of an over (because the chances of his popping up a catch would be increased). The bowler should attempt to pitch the ball in line with (or just outside) the off stump. (This is valid for inswing bowlers.) For an outswing bowler, the target should be to pitch the ball in line with the middle stump or off stump (see Fig.2.3). (These analogies can also be extended to off spinners and leg spinners.) In this context, the example of Sir Richard Hadlee is worth mentioning. He was highly successful because his line and length were absolutely perfect and the batsmen had to play each and every delivery.

One important aspect which governs line and length pertains to the position from which the bowler releases the ball. On even, flat pitches, with little movement in the air or off the pitch, the ball will continue in the same direction after pitching, whether the bowler releases the ball from close to the stumps or from wide off the crease. I have always held the belief that one should bowl from close to the stumps to achieve more accurate line and length. A case in point pertains to former Pakistan captain Imran Khan. I remember facing him in 1978, when he was rather fast, but was bowling from wide off the crease. As a result, he was not very successful. Although he could generate a fair amount of pace and could swing the ball, it would frequently miss the stump. Imran, however, changed his position in 1982, when he started bowling from closer to the stumps. He became not only more accurate but also more devastating, with an amazing degree of control.

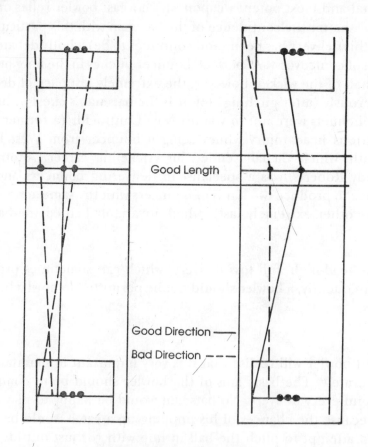

Fig.2.3 Giving direction to bowling

Under conditions wherein the ball tends to swing in the air and seam off the pitch, I still believe that the bowlers should bowl close to the wickets to have control. Variation will always be a key factor in intelligent bowling. One has to skilfully use the bowling crease to achieve variation in bowling in order to surprise a batsman. Using the crease effectively gives different angles to different deliveries. All great bowlers never bowl from the same spot all the time. The more you use the bowling crease strategically, the more doubt you create in a batsman's mind. When you are bowling to a competent batsman, a lot of thinking and planning should go into your deliveries so that you can outwit him and claim his wicket. This is only possible if you have control over direction and length.

You should constantly bear in mind the fact that if you bowl wide off the crease, you will obtain a large amount of inswing. As you move closer to the wicket to bowl, the swing will become progressively lesser. The same rule applies in the case of off spin. Another important factor to be noted is that bowling leg spin, left arm spin around the wicket or outswing from a spot close to the wicket will help the ball move out (after pitching), i.e., away from the batsman and bowling from the edge of crease will help it move in, i.e., towards the batsman.

It has been observed that most right-hand bowlers bowl from *over the wicket* in order to achieve better line and length and also to get a better control over the delivery. This is valid in the cases of bowling to both right-hand and left-hand batsmen. A bowler switches to *around the wicket* only under certain conditions (such as high humidity or a damp pitch) or to change the angle of delivery to. In this context, the example of the Windies paceman Malcolm Marshall is illustrative. Marshall bowled around the wicket to the Indian batsmen in the 1982-83 series with great success.

Slow left arm spinners tend to bowl around the wicket to achieve maximum control over flight and direction. However, one should not hesitate to experiment with unorthodox styles and variations if the circumstances so demand.

FLIGHT

The term 'flight' refers to the upward projection of the ball from the bowler's hand (as opposed to downward projection) at the instant of delivery. Thus, we frequently hear or come across the term 'flighted delivery' especially when a spinner is operating. An effective spinner uses the 'flight' phenomenon as a deceptive means of entrapping his victim. The really intelligent bowler can vary his flight pattern by releasing the ball at different positions in the arc of his bowling arm. Figure 2.4 demarcates different categories of flighted and non-flighted deliveries.

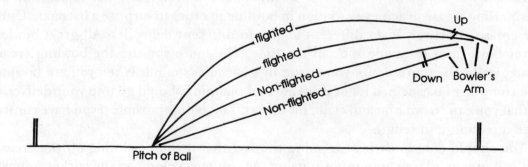

Fig.2.4 Flighted and non-flighted deliveries

Three
Right off the Bat!

THE IMPORTANCE OF ATTITUDE
Before discussing the topic of batting in detail let us dwell upon the right frame of mind needed to perform to the best of one's abilities. Attitude plays a very important part in achieving success. Some highly gifted Indian players could not reach the top because of their negative attitude, whereas less talented players could do so because of their positive attitude. The perfect combination would, of course, be of both talent and attitude.

I am sure every cricketer — young or old — must have a dream of playing the ultimate innings of his life, slamming the bowlers all over the ground with a glittering array of strokes. In reality, such an innings rarely occurs, and when it does, it is a spectacular event. I had the privilege of playing in the Indian team which won the 1983 World Cup. In a particular match against Zimbabwe, at Turnsbridge Wells, Kapil Dev exhibited his batting prowess in a grand style. Undaunted by the fact that we had lost our best batsmen for a paltry score, when he went into bat, he virtually single-handedly turned the game around and led India from the brink of defeat to a resounding victory. Kapil's positive attitude was the motivating factor behind his success.

Vivian Richards, the former West Indies captain, played a resplendent innings for his side in their match against England at Old Trafford. The situation of the Windies was somewhat similar to that of India against Zimbabwe. Here, Richards came to the rescue of his team with a magnificent knock of 189. Again, positive attitude performed wonders.

Other examples of positive attitude include England's Ian Botham's innings against Australia at Headingly (Leeds) in, the 1980-81 series and Pakistan's Javed Miandad's last-ball six off Chetan Sharma at Sharjah in 1986.

UNDERSTANDING ONE'S CAPABILITIES AND WEAKNESSES
I have come across many average batsmen who have exhibited consistently good batting performances over a period of weeks or even months. But, suddenly, on a particular

day, during a crucial phase, they try to change character and attempt such strokes which are really beyond their range and ability. Most probably such batsmen were driven to execute strokes beyond their calibre because they were inspired to imitate some other great batsman, whom they have admired or have seen on the TV, when he was in superb form. In so doing, they lose their wicket. Sometimes, the frustrated players indulge in astonishing self-deceit and start blaming the wickets, the umpire, the light, the weather, the crowd, the pressure of the situation or their own bat or kit. Sometimes, they give due credit to the bowler, but very rarely do the batsmen admit their own mistakes. The point I am trying to make is that every batsman must understand his own capabilities and also limitations and accordingly develop his batting technique.

A serious problem that many cricketers face is being guided into a style of play for which they are not suited either physically or mentally. Always assess your own capabilities, both physical and attitudinal. You sometimes find a well-built, huge bloke with a fiery temperament bowling gentle spin! On the other hand, a short, feeble-looking fellow, with a docile nature, may try to bowl fast-paced deliveries. Such contradictory features not only appear incongruous but also adversely affect one's approach to the game. In other words, try to mould your game according to your physical and mental characteristics and not vice versa.

Some general observations can be made regarding physical traits. For instance, tall batsmen tend to drive the ball exceedingly well, by using the top hand to control and guide their shots. On the other hand, short batsmen tend to have a proclivity for cutting and pulling, i.e., they have a strong bottom hand. Of course, there are exceptions. India's Sunil Gavaskar, though short, could execute amazingly magnificent drives and the fairly tall West Indian Clive Lloyd could pull the ball almost effortlessly.

On can also develop one's batting technique and skill by emulating great batsmen. For instance, Sir Donald Bradman, Sir Garfield Sobers, Vivian Richards, Allan Border, G.R. Vishwanath, Sunil Gavaskar, David Gower, Javed Miandad, Sachin Tendulkar and Brian Lara offer role models. One can learn a lot about stroke play by reading about or carefully watching in action the aforementioned luminaries of the cricket world.

The state of the wicket and climatic conditions make a tremendous impact on the players. Batsmen from the West Indies, Asia and Australia tend to be free flowing stroke players because of the hard wickets in their region and also because of the effect of the weather. The repertoire of strokes of these batsmen is varied. On the other hand, English batsmen generally concentrate more on their push drives because there the balls tend to move more in the air and off the seam. The 'straight bat' represented the hallmark of a distinguished band of English batsmen such as Jack Hobbs, Herbert Sutcliffe, Len Hutton, Walter Hammond, Collin Cowdrey and Geoff Boycott. These players were masters of both front foot and back foot play.

Other legendary cricketers such as Sir Don Bradman, Sir Garfield Sobers, Rohan Kanhai, the Chappell Brothers (Ian and Greg), Sunil Gavaskar, Clive Lloyd, Alvin Kalicharan, Vivian Richards, Gordon Greenidge, Javed Miandad and Allan Border could also play with ease both of the front foot and back foot.

In this context, batsmen should analyse their own capabilities and shortcomings, discuss them with other teammates and their coach and then finally decide the technique to adopt. By concentrating on a few types of strokes and by executing them perfectly, a batsman can definitely improve his game and develop a positive attitude, rather than trying out too many strokes and not being able to master any of them, thereby leading to wasted effort and lack of results. Let me cite a few relevant examples. The West Indian opener Gordon Greenidge was undoubtedly an all-round stroke player; however, during the early part of his innings, he would concentrate on playing only a few types of strokes to maximum effect. Any ball pitched short would be despatched to the ropes with tremendous power. Next, let us take the examples of Sunil Gavaskar and Ravi Shastri. Gavaskar would begin his innings very cautiously, playing a limited number of strokes. Of course, once he got set, there was no stopping him. Ravi Shastri, despite his limited range of stroke play, but because he attained perfection in playing them effectively and also because of his positive attitude, was able to achieve a lot at the international level.

During my cricketing career, I have been involved in several partnerships with Sunil Gavaskar. By studying his batting technique, I managed to pick up quite a few valuable points. Most importantly, he would play his strokes very close to the body and lean into his shots rather than smashing them violently. Therefore, it is always worthwhile to keep your eyes open and watch the other batsman playing. One can do so also as a fielder, especially when positioned close to the bat and, sometimes, also from the outfield.

I have always disliked (and been wary of) batsmen who have scored 'theoretical' centuries in the dressing room without even stepping into the middle. One must remember that the real game involves not only two batsmen and eleven fielders but also the two umpires. In other words, a batsman can prove his mettle only *on* the cricketing field, amidst the 'rough-and-tumble' activities, and not by indulging in 'flights of fancy'.

Most batsmen are overcautious when facing their first delivery. Different batsmen cope with the first ball differently, depending on their individual characteristics and also on the prevailing situation of the game. Many batsmen take their own time in carefully surveying the trajectory of the ball, the pace of the wicket and the bowlers' style. They avoid playing strokes initially, focussing more on defending their wickets. In my opinion, the best and positive approach is to get off the mark, and score runs as quickly as possible in order to gain confidence. In fact, many great batsmen open their account with a single or two runs, so as to overcome their early nervousness. If a batsman gets stuck on zero itself, even after facing a lot of deliveries, his confidence would be eroded. I would suggest that you play your natural game right from the beginning, provided you have perfected your strokes and are determined to make a positive effort. One should develop the power of thinking and then tackling the bowling. A tactical-minded, thinking batsman can often make a tremendous impact, whereas a gifted but non-thinking batsman may fall into a rut; although he may be playing classic shots, they tend to go the same place, over and over again, with the result that he is not able to pierce the field. Also, out of frustration, he may play an erroneous shot and get out. In other words, an ideal batsman should be able to adapt to the situation rapidly.

In order to outfox and also to pressurise a batsman into committing errors, the opposing captain will adjust his field accordingly. A non-thinking batsman could become an easy victim of a stupid shot. On the other hand, a thinking batsman would carefully survey the field placement and assess the ability of each fielder, and play his strokes accordingly. In this category of players, I would like to include the two outstanding Pakistani cricketers Javed Miandad and Imran Khan. They have led their team to victory several times as a result of shrewd tactical planning and positive thinking.

Another significant feature of batting which needs to be emphasised pertains to *running between the wickets.* The batsmen should utilise every opportunity to place the ball and dart across for a single or two, so that the scoreboard can keep moving. Such a strategy would be imperative in cases where boundaries or sixers cannot be easily hit, especially if the outfield is slow or wet. The respective duo of batsmen should chalk out their plan of action after discussing with the captain and other senior teammates. Much would naturally depend on the weather conditions, the state of the pitch, the target being chased or aimed at, the number of wickets in hand, and the quality and ability of the opposing team's bowlers and fielders.

Ideally, a great deal of planning has to be done before the game commences. The team members (obviously the captain included) should be able to identify the strong points and shortcomings of the rival team and develop their strategy accordingly. Of course, such a strategy has to be flexible to allow for a good deal of change and improvisation in tactics as the match progresses. In the 1991 World Cup matches between New Zealand and Pakistan, the Pakistan batsman Inzamam-ul Haq played a calculated innings and helped Pakistan in reaching the finals. (Pakistan ultimately won the World Cup.) A similar knock was played by Wasim Akram (also of Pakistan) which enabled his team to achieve victory (against India at Sharjah in 1989), despite the fact that they were chasing a stiff target. It is a common belief that 'bowlers win matches'. I do not agree completely with this because without the batsmen's efforts and contribution no team can attain victory.

Before we move on to study in detail the skills and techniques involved in batting, I would like to express my firm conviction that batsmen invariably get themselves out by playing a wrong stroke to a particular delivery. (Of course, very few will acknowledge this fact!) My suggestion is that whenever one falls victim to such a stroke, one should ponder over it and try to analyse the reasons for making a mistake. You should remember that all the practice in the world would not be good enough if you are unable to perfect your strokes. An alert and fast-learning batsman does not repeat his mistakes;

i.e., does not fall victim twice to the same erroneous stroke. In my cricketing dictionary, there is no such thing as an 'unplayable delivery'. A competent batsman treats every delivery according to its merit. He would respect all good deliveries and play them carefully and, contrarily, he would punish all bad deliveries. Such a batsman must have the ability to identify which delivery is good length, half volley or long hop and execute his stroke accordingly. For example, he should pull a short-pitched delivery; or he should offer a defensive bat to a good length delivery pitched on the middle stump.

It sometimes happens that a batsman 'goes out of form' or 'strikes a bad patch', i.e., even under ideal batting conditions, he is unable to score runs. In such a situation, a knowledgeable coach or other teammates would pay attention to three basic factors, namely, grip, stance and back lift. I recollect playing against the West Indies in India in the 1983-84 series. I could score only one run in six innings — a dismal performance indeed! I went in for some self-introspection and self-analysis, and came to the conclusion that the three abovementioned factors were the 'culprits' behind my débâcle. One other significant factor, usually not paid much attention to, is the weight of the bat. If a batsman does not play with a correct weight bat suited to his specific abilities, he could get into serious trouble. For instance, if a lean and wiry batsman chooses an extra-heavy bat, he would not be able to play his strokes with precise timing (he would be late in executing his strokes).

The general 'rule of thumb' is that a front foot player would find a heavy bat suitable and a back foot player would prefer a light bat. This is because a front foot player normally pushes or drives forward, whereas a back foot player pulls, hooks or cuts, i.e., a light bat would provide a better back lift. A batsman's physique could also determine the type of bat needed. A burly, robust and tall player would naturally prefer a heavy bat and a light-weight batsman would opt for a light bat. In conclusion, I would state that the 'right choice' of a bat would depend on a combination of factors, determined by each individual player's capabilities, build and needs.

GETTING THE RIGHT GRIP
Let us now dwell on the 'grip' factor. If a batsman were to score runs slowly the critics would attribute it to his peculiar 'grip'. I do believe in the traditional, old-fashioned way of playing cricket, but I am not against improvisation or modification, depending on the situation of the game and the batsman's abilities or idiosyncrasies. I feel it is better to learn to play in the orthodox manner for building a strong foundation. However, if a batsman has an unorthodox grip and still manages to amass runs he should not change his grip because it would then affect his natural talent (which is a God-given gift).

In the orthodox grip, both hands should be close together, with the left hand on top gripping the handle firmly and the right hand below, comparatively loose *vis-à-vis* the left hand. The gap between both hands should not be more than one inch. A 'V' is formed by the first finger and thumb (of both hands), which should be in the same line and pointing between the splice and the outside edge of the bat (see Fig.3.1). (Approximately one inch of the handle should be visible above the left hand.)

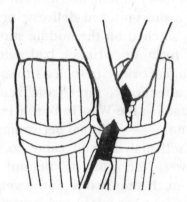

Fig 3.1 Getting the ideal grip

Normally, a driver of the ball would have his 'Vs' close to the outside edge of the bat so as to facilitate his wrist to move freely in order to execute the drive shot or play the defensive stroke comfortably. For the check drive (also known as 'forward push') and defensive play, the batsmen normally keep their 'Vs' in the line of splice, which restricts their follow through. I would suggest that the grip of the 'V' should be in the middle of the splice and the outside edge to enable the batsman to play strokes and defend well at the same time.

Some players adopt an unorthodox grip; for instance, one hand would hold the top of the handle and the other the bottom. Nevertheless, they may be able to play their strokes comfortably and effectively. Into this category fall Javed Miandad and Asif Iqbal, who were exceptionally talented players.

I used to change my grip while playing against pace and spin in order to control my strokes. Against genuine pace and sometimes against medium fast stuff, my right hand would be near the bottom of the handle and the left hand close by. I would hold the handle with a firm grip because, against quick bowlers, it becomes necessary to control the shots as most of their deliveries are short in length and one could play with more authority off the back foot, specially strokes such as square cut, pull and hook.

When playing off the front foot, you need not hit the ball hard because even a check drive or a push will fetch you runs. You may not be able to smash the ball very hard, but, again, the basic idea is to score runs. I always found that holding the bat in a slightly lower grip gives one better control.

THE PERFECT STANCE

Just like the grip, a batsman's stance should be comfortable and well balanced. Different successful batsmen have adopted different kinds of stance. If you are facing problems with regard to stance, then it is better you adopt the traditional stance. Irrespective of a batsman's other qualities, such as style and application, without proper stance, his performance would be limited. The following points should be noted with respect to the traditional stance (see Fig.3.2):

Fig.3.2 Taking stance: side view and front view

1. As far as possible the position of the feet should be parallel to the batting crease; or else the front left toe could be pointing towards the cover position.* The right foot should remain inside the crease and the left foot outside the crease.
2. The feet should be placed comfortably apart (6" to 12") and the weight should be evenly balanced, so that the batsman can move quickly on the front foot or back foot. If the feet are too close to each other, free movement would be restricted. On the other hand, too wide a stance could also reduce one's mobility. Nevertheless there are exceptions and the prominent example is that of K. Srikkanth, who plants his feet very wide apart and thus is forced to crouch a bit. This stance, he maintains, is useful against quick bowling because one does have to move much. Of course, in order to adopt Srikkanth's stance, you must possess his incredibly swift reflexes, otherwise you could land up in all sorts of trouble!
3. The body weight should *never* rest on your heels as this will slow down your movement. Both knees should be lightly flexed so that one can move quickly whenever required, with the left hip slightly more open than the left shoulder. The bat should be resting close to the right toe.
4. The back of the left hand should be facing a point between the covers and mid-off and should rest on the left thigh, touching the inside of the front pad and the right hand should rest lightly against the flap of the right pad or right thigh.

---

* See Chapter 4 for the various fielding positions.

5. The left shoulder should face the line of the wickets at the non-striker's end or should be angled towards the mid-on position.
6. When a left hand bowler is bowling over the wicket, you should open your left shoulder a bit more to get a better view of the bowler. However, if a right hand bowler switches to round the wicket or a left arm bowler bowls over the wicket, the batsman could change the position of his feet slightly. Instead of keeping the feet parallel to the batting crease, he could open his left hip slightly, with the left toe opening up more and facing towards extra cover.
7. The head should be turned fully to face the bowler, with both eyes on level as far as possible and the left chin staying as close to the left shoulder as possible.
8. One should try to stand as erect as possible so that one can move freely because too much crouching restricts one's movements. If someone has to copy an ideal stance then there isn't a better stance in cricketing history than Sunil Gavaskar's. You should see how perfectly positioned he is when standing and how well placed his body weight is, with his arms fully relaxed.

Even a slight shift in the body weight can help you in tackling pace quite easily and comfortably. Put more weight on your left or front foot so that you can move your back foot quickly and handle the short stuff with ease. Do just the opposite when facing spinners; put more weight on the right foot so that the left foot stays free and you can come out of the crease to tackle spin comfortably as you will be playing more off the front foot against spin. Change your grip and hold the handle of the bat near the top with the left hand, with right hand staying close to the left hand (when both hands are together). This grip would help you to play your front foot strokes more freely with a good swing and a better reach and the left hand would be controlling the bat.

There is a popular saying in cricket that one should keep one's head steady and play the ball late if one wants to be in a good position to play shots. The 'head' plays a crucial role in all aspects of the game, especially in batting. In other words, one should remain cool and composed to the extent possible so that one could watch the ball till the last second and then execute an appropriate stroke. Here, 'play the ball late' does not mean that one has to move slowly; what this means is that one should make some allowance for swing or spin, study the movement of the ball carefully and then decide on the stroke to be played. In reality, all these activities have to be performed in a matter of seconds. Consequently, perfect judgement, quick reflexes and instant decision-making acumen are imperative.

Even before the bowler releases the ball, virtually every batsman is subjected to some slight initial movement. Whenever I faced the quick bowlers, I always had a slight backward movement, just before the bowler released the ball, which enabled me to gain those vital extra seconds needed for executing my back foot strokes, especially the hook. Such initial movement, forward or backward, helps a batsman in adjusting his position in order to play his shots confidently and effectively.

The batting activity has to be carried out side-on in order to play one's strokes correctly. This is possible only if the head stays close to the left shoulder, the initial movement of the feet is not much and the bat is lifted straight. Those who cannot maintain the side-on position should open up their stance, i.e., the left shoulder should point towards mid-on, so that their eyes are level and can see both the bowler and the ball properly. However, in case a player adopts an open stance, he has to move his left shoulder quickly towards the off side, in the line of the ball, in order to execute his stroke comfortably and efficiently.

I do not attach too much importance to mere theoretical discussion or 'armchair strategies'. As long as you are able to middle the ball and hit it as desired, you can forget about theories and speculative 'do's and don't's'. I would like to reiterate that if you feel comfortable and confident with an unorthodox stance, and can score runs fluently, do not change your stance.

I changed my stance in 1982-83, when I was recalled for the Pakistan tour. I adopted a fairly open stance. Even my feet were not parallel to the batting crease (my right toe was facing the covers and my left toe was facing extra covers). However, at the time of tackling the delivery, I used to turn my shoulder towards the off side and shift my feet so that they became parallel to the batting crease. As a matter of fact, I was playing more side-on than any other batsman, but I was termed as the 'batsman with the two-eyed stance'. I would like to point out that every stance is a two-eyed stance; otherwise how can one see both the bowler and the ball in the proper perspective? An open chested stance is particularly useful in effectively tackling short pitched deliveries.

Very few batsmen have achieved success with the open stance or two-eyed stance. The two cricketers who immediately come to mind are Ken Barrington (England) and Javed Miandad (Pakistan).

TAKING GUARD

Before facing his first delivery, every batsman has to 'take guard'. This activity enables him to know exactly where he shall be standing in front of the wickets, without looking backward, when he is ready to face the bowler. In order to take guard, first of all, the batsman holds the bat vertically in front of the wickets, with the bottom of the bat resting on the ground. He then asks the umpire to 'give him guard', either with respect to the middle or leg stump. Once the umpire has signalled the precise position, the batsman makes a light mark at that point with the edge of the bat or with his spike shoes. Every batsman should make sure (by checking and rechecking) that his toes touch the marked point before facing any delivery.

It is obvious that every batsman will have his own 'guard-taking' mark. Generally, most Indian batsmen prefer the leg stump (or the leg-and-middle stump guard), whereas overseas players opt for the middle stump (or the middle and leg stump) guard. The basic difference that I have noticed between the two guards is that if you take the leg stump guard, you tend to play your strokes much straighter and if you take the middle stump guard, you tend to play more on the leg side.

Of course, a lot depends on where the ball is pitched, how much foot movement is required and how much across the batsman is playing. For example, Sunil Gavaskar used to take the leg stump guard and would take his stance slightly away from it because against fast bowlers he used to step back a bit (and across) to judge the line of the ball accurately. If Gavaskar had stood in the middle and had to move his feet to execute his shot, I am sure he would have faced problems in judging the line properly. I am not suggesting that you should imitate Gavaskar; I am merely citing an ideal example. Depending your foot movement ability, you should take guard accordingly.

BACK LIFT

One of the most important aspects of batting is the *back lift*. (See Fig. 3.3.) As a matter of fact, a batsman's life at the crease depends on his back lift. Whenever critics and commentators try to analyse why, at times, even accomplished batsmen get out cheaply or strike a 'bad patch', they attribute the cause to back lift, which can 'make' or 'break' a batsman.

Fig 3.3 Back lift illustrated: side view and front view

During the course of my career, both 'ups' and 'downs' were inevitably there. I had a memorable and outstanding series against the West Indies and Pakistan in 1982-83. I could score runs fluently against the fairly intimidating pace attack of Malcolm Marshall, Michael Holding, Joel Garner, Andy Roberts and Imran Khan. Nothing seemed to bother me, and I was able to middle the ball perfectly. I was able to play positive cricket because of a proper and straight back lift. (As a matter of record, I scored around 600 runs in each of the series against West Indies and Pakistan.) Then came the shocking nightmare of my career. I was struggling to score even a single run against the West Indies in the home series. I was naturally depressed and dejected and could not readily figure out the reason for my inability to do well. Finally, after a good deal of analysis and introspection, I came to the conclusion that the 'culprit' was my back lift. Instead of being straight, my back lift was aimed towards the second or third slip positions (or even gully). As a result, I was playing across, leaving a gap between bat and pad. Thus, one should always remember that it becomes very difficult to strike the ball effectively without a technically perfect back lift (see Fig. 3.3).

The following points should be constantly borne in mind in order to achieve a perfect back lift:

1. The top hand (i.e., left hand) must take control.
2. The back lift must be commenced before any other movement, so that you can play your strokes easily.
3. Your front forearm should be almost parallel to the ground, with the wrist positioned higher than the elbow and the right hand being higher than the left hand.
4. You should keep your head absolutely still.
5. Keep your elbows slightly away from the body in order to enable free movement, which, in turn, would ensure a good back lift.
6. The left shoulder should stay under the chin (or close to the chin), with the face fully turned towards the bowler and the eyes focussed on the bowler's hands.
7. Take your front arm backwards to attain a high back lift.
8. Allow the wrists to cock naturally so as to open the face of the bat.
9. Pick your bat up in the line of the wickets.

Some of the successful batsmen (e.g., Zaheer Abbas of Pakistan and Mohammed Azharuddin of India) have tended to pick their bat up between the first and second slip positions with a big 'loop' at the top. When they commit themselves to play a stroke, they bring the bat down straight and watch the ball carefully, through the line of stroke. Such batsmen have proved to be excellent players square of the wickets, on both sides, but more on the leg side.

Other important factors to be noted in order to attain a straight back lift are as follows: (1) the batsman should bend his knees a bit when he is about to receive the ball; (2) the weight should be more on the toes than the heels; and (3) the left elbow joint should face the wickets at the other end. All these factors enable the batsman to swing the bat properly, with the left shoulder in line with the ball.

If you find that you are facing problems with your back lift, you can try out this simple procedure in order to improve and correct it. Draw a straight line on the ground with a piece of chalk, and place your feet parallel to this line. Hold your bat with your left hand at the top of the handle. The base of the bat should remain near your right toe. Next, lift the bat with the top (left) hand, take it back to a high position and swing it forward straight and keep on repeating the backward and forward movements as many times as possible. This will help improve your back lift and help in keeping your bat straight. You can perform this 'experiment' in front of a full-length mirror and ask somebody to watch and pinpoint the exact position of the back lift and, if defective, you could rectify it suitably.

SUMMING UP

I have explained the basics of batting, i.e., the grip, the stance, the guard and the back lift. The basic function of a batsman is to score runs and keep up the tempo of the game. Nevertheless, one has to play defensive strokes at times, however much one would like to go in for attacking shots.

The importance of hard work and regular practice can hardly be overemphasized. A batsman should possess an array of both defensive and attacking strokes and also a sound technique, so that he can stay at the crease for a long time and also keep the scoreboard ticking. Let us now discuss the various kinds of strokes (or shots) individually.

THE FORWARD DEFENSIVE STROKE

The forward defensive stroke (Fig. 3.4) proves extremely useful while facing seamers or spinners, especially on a turning wicket. Players from England are usually sound in their defence, because of the weather conditions there which assist seam bowling,

Fig. 3.4 The forward defensive stroke position

especially the inswingers and outswingers. On the other hand, Indian and Pakistani batsmen can tackle spin with ease because they are accustomed to playing on dry, turning wickets. Such generalisations apart, one needs to cultivate a reliable defensive technique, irrespective of the kind of wicket. In this regard, two outstanding batsmen come to my mind, namely, Sunil Gavaskar and G.R. Vishwanath. In the 1988-89 series against Pakistan, at Bangalore, Gavaskar tackled the spinners so easily that players from both sides were surprised as to how he could do it because he was basically considered as a proficient player of fast bowling! This particular match was played on a 'wicket that wasn't'. Despite the fact that the ball bounced, jumped, kicked and turned enormously, Gavaskar managed to achieve remarkable feats of batsmanship.

Javed Miandad is another great player who is not only a tremendous stroke player but also a great grafter. His defence is as effective as his stroke play. Allan Border, Geoff Boycott, Glen Turner, Dilip Vengsarkar and

Gordon Greenidge are some of the others known for their defensive stroke play also. The following points need to be noted as regards forward defensive play (see Fig. 3.4):

1. You don't need a very high back lift for this stroke because, in this case, you have to just stop the ball. Some of the players don't use any back lift at all. Professionals such as Viv Richards and Kalicharan had a minimum of back lift for this kind of stroke.
2. Your front foot and the bat should move together and the left leg should go into the line of the ball. One should lead with the front shoulder and the head should be kept inside the line of the ball.
3. Your front shoulder and head should stay together and the eyes should remain on the ball because it's important to observe carefully the line of the delivery.
4. The body weight should be placed entirely on the front foot; the back leg should be fully extended and should stay inside the crease.
5. Bat and pad should stay together so that you don't leave any gap between them.
6. The bat should be angled forward by a firm top hand grip (but not too tight) with the bottom hand playing a supporting role; the thumb and forefingers should be loose.
7. You should lean on the stroke and should bend your back as well. You should keep your head down. When you play this stroke your left elbow should stay high, keeping the bat vertical (straight).
8. The head should be positioned well forward, looking down at the ball.

Common Mistakes during Forward Defensive Play
1. Many batsmen do not lean on the stroke properly. As a consequence, they tend to be away from the ball, which takes the edge of the bat and results in a catch to the close-in fielders. The cardinal rule is: never allow the ball to come to you; you should reach the ball first.
2. Lots of players do not go to the pitch of the ball. Also, they do not take strides long enough to reach the ball or they tend to play over the ball or they do not move much and play the ball half-cock.
3. Many batsmen do not bend their back at all; i.e., they tend to remain stiff and rigid.
4. Several batsmen do not keep their eyes on the ball, with the result that in a last-ditch effort to save their wicket, they commit errors.
5. Some batsmen tend to move too early to play forward, even before correctly judging the line and length of the ball.

FORWARD PUSH OR CHECK DRIVE

Forward push and *check drive* are merely two different names given to the same stroke. This stroke proves to be a much safer 'defence mechanism' than the forward defensive stroke. This is because a batsman has to use less force while playing this stroke, but the effects are the same. This stroke is also known as the 'bread and butter' stroke since it is played with a great deal of caution. I would definitely recommend this stroke under those conditions wherein the ball tends to seam or swing a lot.

The forward push is normally played to a delivery which lands close a batsman's left foot. Unlike the forward defence, in this case, the bat is pushed forward. The left shoulder leads the batsman into the stroke, and the left foot goes near the pitch of the ball.

For the forward push, a high back lift is needed (more than that for the forward defensive stroke). However, this stroke has a limited follow through. When playing the forward push, the weight of the body rests on the front foot (as the stroke is played off the front foot). The front knee (left) is bent and the head is normally kept down, with the eyes focussed on the ball. The back should also be bent forward so that the shot can be well timed with a minimum of effort.

A lot of batsmen in England resort to the forward push frequently, because of the weather conditions and the type of wickets there. At present, this stroke is also in vogue because many players prefer to use heavy bats (mainly for their power), which at times, they find difficult to wield and to complete their follow through.

The various forward strokes are illustrated in Fig. 3.5.

THE DRIVE

The drive is an elegant and graceful stroke and a delight to watch, especially if executed by proficient batsmen such as Clive Lloyd, Vivian Richards, Zaheer Abbas, Sunil Gavaskar, Ian Botham, Alan Border, Dean Jones, Kim Hughes, David Gower, Graham Gooch, Salim Malik, Mohammed Azharuddin and the young but brilliant Sachin Tendulkar. These renowned batsmen played (and some of them continue to play) this stroke with a minimum of effort. Nevertheless, the ball invariably sped (or speeds) to the boundary like a rocket! I still recall Viv Richards' beautiful drives against English bowlers in 1976 and also Botham's glorious almost single-handed match-winning effort against Australia in 1980. The power of Lloyd's drives was legendary. In fact, several times, fielders stationed right on the boundary line could not stop the ball from crossing it. All these players did not achieve success overnight; they had to strive hard for years.

The drive is normally played to a delivery pitching well up to the batsman on or just outside the off stump.

The drive follows all the initial movements of a forward defensive stroke, but the difference here is that the back lift becomes very high because the batsman would really like to smash the ball. One wallops the ball on the half volley. The moment he

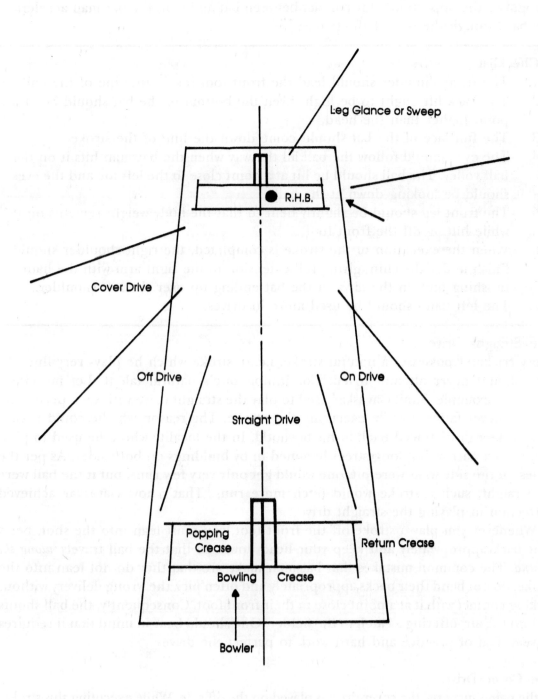

Fig. 3.5 The various forward strokes

recognises the opportunity for contact between bat and ball, the batsman accelerates the bat through the line of the stroke.

Checklist

1. The front shoulder should lead the front foot inside the line of the ball.
2. The back lift ought to be high. Even the bottom of the bat should be at a point higher than the head.
3. The full face of the bat should come down the line of the stroke.
4. The eyes should follow the ball all the way when the batsman hits it on the half volley. The ball should be hit at a point close to the left toe and the eyes should be looking down at the ball.
5. The front leg should be slightly bent so that the body weight remains on it while hitting off the front foot.
6. When the execution of the stroke is completed, the right shoulder should finish under the chin, giving full extension to the right arm with the hands finishing high in the air and the bat ending up over the left shoulder.
7. The left hand should be used more in drives.

The Straight Drive

Every cricketer possesses a natural stroke, i.e., a stroke which he plays very fluently. One should never attempt to curb or inhibit one's natural talent. Let me cite a pertinent example. Sunil Gavaskar used to play the straight drive with such perfection that he never faltered while executing this stroke. The reason why he could master this stroke can be traced back to his boyhood. In the locality where he used to play, there was a narrow but long street hemmed in by buildings on both sides. As per the 'rules', if the side walls were hit, one would get only very few runs, but if the ball were hit straight, such a stroke would fetch more runs. That's how Gavaskar achieved perfection in playing the straight drive.

Whenever you play a stroke off the front foot, you must lean into the shot, bend your back appropriately and keep your head down, so that the ball travels *along the ground*. The common mistakes that batsmen make are that they do not lean into the stroke, do not bend their backs appropriately and often pick the wrong delivery without making contact with it at a point close to their front foot. Consequently, the ball shoots up into the air, offering a catch to the fielder. One should bear in mind that it requires a great deal of practice and hard work to perfect the drive.

The Cover Drive

As the name suggests, the cover drive is played on the off side. While executing this stroke, the batsman's left shoulder is turned more (towards the off side) in line with the wider delivery. Here, the left shoulder plays an important role, because even the back lift is connected to it (Fig. 3.6). For example, if you want to play the cover drive and if your shoulder remains straight and stiff, this situation will cause problems for you. The reason why many batsmen are not comfortable while playing the outgoing delivery (for a cover drive) is that they are unable to turn their left shoulder towards the off side, resulting in their spooning up an easy catch to the wicket-keeper or the slips.

One has to be very cautious in the beginning while tackling the swinging or turning deliveries. As I have earlier suggested, the batsman must lean into the stroke to achieve precision and control.

Checklist

1. The front foot should reach the pitch of the ball. The ball should be taken on the half volley and the left shoulder should turn more in the line of the ball, with the bat coming from the leg slip position to the fine leg position. The precise angle would depend on how square or fine the batsman intends to play the stroke. The left knee should be bent, the batsman should lean into the stroke, with the eyes and head kept down.

2. The cover drive requires a high back lift and a smooth follow through. After the cover drive has been completed, the bat ends up over the left shoulder, with the hands high in the air and the right shoulder under the right chin.

3. The batsman could bend both knees while playing the cover drive; i.e., the front leg being slightly bent and the right knee resting close to the ground. However, this pattern of stroke play is valid more while facing spinners. One must maintain good control over the body while playing the cover drive, and stretch the front leg only up to the point wherein one feels comfortable.

Fig. 3.6   The cover drive

I can think of several players who could play the cover drive with ease, authority and perfection. Prominent among them are Sunil Gavaskar, Graham Gooch, Alvin Kalicharan, Walter Hammond, the Chappell Brothers, Viv Richards, Rohan Kanhai, Garfield Sobers, Clive Lloyd, Tom Graveney and Ted Dexter.

(The reason for my mentioning Gavaskar's name repeatedly is because I have had the opportunity of watching him play from very close quarters, at all levels of cricket, for over two decades. He must have played the cover drive on ever so many occasions, but the stroke I still vividly recall pertains to the 1982-83 series against the West Indies at Trinidad. Malcolm Marshall, the West Indies paceman, who was bowling on a green-top wicket, delivered a wide outswinger. Gavaskar executed an exquisite but authoritative cover drive, with the left knee bent, the right knee on the ground, the shoulder in perfect position, head down, eyes on the ball and a lovely follow through. This picture is still imprinted on my mind. Even Marshall applauded the stroke and still talks about it!)

The On Drive

The on drive is not an easy stroke to play mainly because the head seems to fall to the off side while executing this stroke, thus upsetting the body's balance and throwing the bat out of the line of the stroke. This results in an uppish shot being played, with a catch being given to the mid-wicket or short mid-on position. Therefore, proper body balance is essential. Also, the batsman should lean into the shot to guide the ball properly (Fig. 3.7).

West Indian and Australian cricketers are adroit in playing the on drive. (This does not mean that players from other countries cannot play this stroke!) The eminent 'on drivers' include Viv Richards, Greg Chappell, Ken Barrington, Peter May and, inevitably, Sunil Gavaskar.

Fig. 3.7 The on drive

Checklist
1. The left shoulder should be opened out in order to play the ball on the on side.
2. The bat should come straight down or from the first or second slip positions, depending on how straight or wide the batsman intends to play his stroke on the on side.
3. The shoulder (and the head too) should lean over the stroke and remain well balanced in order to play the stroke elegantly.
4. The right hand should be used frequently for this shot.
5. The batsman should play over the ball, striking it close to his left foot.
6. The on drive is normally played to a ball which pitches on the middle or leg stump and comes into the batsman (right-handed).

Some batsmen play the on drive against an outgoing delivery, i.e., one that leaves the bat, with disastrous results. Such a delivery should be played straight. The thumb rule is: incoming deliveries are played on the on side and outgoing deliveries on the off side. Normally, when a batsman tries to play against the swing or spin of the ball, he tends to get into trouble. However, if an exceptionally gifted batsman can play easily and naturally against the swing or spin, there is no reason why he should change his technique. Again, as regards the on drive, constant practice is the key to perfection.

The Lofted Drive

The lofted drive can fetch a batsman a large number of runs, provided he executes the stroke correctly. Another advantage is that this drive upsets the line and rhythm of the bowler, with telling effect, because the deliveries keep getting slammed for fours or heaved for sixes. Before playing the lofted drive, a batsman must survey the field placing carefully. If a player is stationed right on the boundary line, it would be foolish (and sometimes disastrous) to try to hit the ball over his head, if the batsman is not in full control. Although Kapil Dev has gained sufficient proficiency in executing the lofted drive time and time again, on one occasion, he did botch up the stroke. During the 1987 World Cup match against England, Kapil lofted the ball, trying to hit over the boundary fielder's head, and was caught in the bargain. As a result, India lost to England and Kapil lost his captaincy.

The lofted drive is normally played to a full-length delivery which is just short of half volley. This stroke can be played on either side of the wicket or also straight down the wicket, against both pace and spin. The incidence of the lofted drive being played against spin is much higher because of the slow pace and the flight of the ball. The prominent exponents of the lofted drive include Richards, Srikkant, Miandad, Botham, Gooch and Imran Khan. Of late, Brian Lara, Sachin Tendulkar and Vinod Kambli have hogged the limelight. This stroke is more prevalent in one-day cricket compared to test matches because of the urgency of getting quick runs and also due to mandatory close-in fielders. The lofted drive can be played right from the crease, when the batsman brings his front foot forward to hit the ball or else he can move out of his crease to whack the ball (Fig. 3.8).

Fig 3.8 The lofted drive

Checklist
1. For executing the lofted drive, a batsman should follow the same pattern as for the drive. The lofted drive also requires a high back lift, a good swing and a smooth follow through.
2. The batsman's front (left) shoulder and left foot lead him into the shot, and the ball is hit just short of half volley.
3. In this case, the batsman should not lean into the shot but should keep his front leg straight (i.e., without bending the knee).
4. At the time of contact the head should be down and eyes should be focussed on the ball.
5. The back should stay straight, so that the batsman can lift the ball; both hands finish high in the air.

Moving Out to Drive or 'Dancing Down the Wicket'
A batsman normally moves out of his crease to hammer the ball in the case of spin bowling. Enterprising batsmen are not afraid to step out of the crease to tackle the spinners' attack by smothering the spin and applying pressure on the bowler (Fig. 3.9). The batsman must have quick reflexes and even quicker footwork; otherwise, he would be stranded in 'no man's land' if he misses the delivery!

Under ideal conditions and on a sedate wicket, moving down the wicket to hit the ball would prove fruitful. However, on a turning wicket, one has to be cautious in playing from outside the crease. A batsman should step out of his crease *only after* he can accurately determine which way the ball is going to spin and how much. I have seen many batsmen being caught or stumped while attempting to 'dance down the wicket' because they misjudged the line and length of a particular delivery. If a batsman blindly jumps out of his crease to thrash each and every delivery, his life span would be very short indeed. Naturally, the bowler would feel thrilled if he could entice a batsman out of his crease and fox the latter with his flight and spin.

Ian Chappell (of Australia) was a great player against spin, and used his feet very skilfully. He was so light on his feet that, at times, it seemed as if he were walking and dancing above the ground! Sunil Gavaskar (yes, again!) was another batsman who used his feet exceedingly well. The point I'm trying to emphasise is that one has to be absolutely sure about the nature of the wicket and one's confidence to play the spinners before 'dancing down the wicket'. If the batsmen merely leap out of the crease and try to smash every delivery, they will land up in serious trouble. The West Indies faced such a situation at Madras in the 1987-88 series. In this match, leg spinner Narendra Hirwani amassed 16 wickets on a turning wicket. He kept on bowling flighted deliveries consistently with a good line, and the West Indies batsmen kept on playing against the spin and either popped up catches or were stumped.

A 'dancing down the wicket' stroke can be played on the off side, leg side or straight down the wicket. Due allowance has to be made for the amount of spin before deciding whether to play on the off side or on side.

Fig. 3.9 Moving out to drive

Checklist

1. Whenever a batsman steps out of his crease, he should do so with the intention of hitting the ball forcefully; he should check his stroke only if he has no other choice.

2. The batsman's first stride (out of the crease) should be as long as possible in the line of the ball. The back foot (right) should come parallel behind the front foot (left) and the next step should be in the line of the pitch of the delivery. The batsman should try to make contact with the ball close to the left foot, so that it can be hit along the ground.

3. The left shoulder leads in the stroke play. The batsman must have a high back lift and must maintain a sideways position *vis-à-vis* the wickets on the opposite side. This is possible only if the batsman's first movement is parallel to the batting crease (i.e., left foot parallel to the batting crease) so that he can play easily on the off side (to a delivery pitched on or outside the off stump).

4. When the bat makes contact with the ball, the batsman's head should be down, with the eyes on the ball. The front knee should be bent and the batsman should play the stroke in a manner similar to the drive with a smooth follow through.

5. The batsman should always play with a positive attitude (sorry for the repetition). He should leave the crease only after having sighted the ball and read the bowler's hand, i.e., after having determined the ball's line and amount of spin in it. Once the batsman has stepped out of the crease, he can convert a good length delivery into a half volley and a half volley into a full toss.

6. The ideal way to play spin is to exert less weight on your front foot, so that you can move easily, without much hindrance.

7. The bat should be held high, i.e., the handle should be held at a spot near the top. Such a grip would provide more reach and help you in driving on the on side.

8. For playing the on side drive, the batsman should follow the same steps (mentioned earlier), the only difference being that he should open up his left shoulder. The batsman should not maintain a side-on position for on side stroke play. The batsman's first stride should be, as long as possible, in the line of the delivery. The right foot, instead of coming behind the left foot, should remain straight, next to the left foot. Next, the left foot should be taken to the pitch of the ball and the on drive should be executed with a high back lift a good swing and a smooth follow through.

9. The batsman should keep his head (and eyes) down while playing the on drive because the head invariably tends to fall a little to the off side.

No spinner really enjoys bowling to batsmen who use their feet effectively because this upsets both their rhythm and their confidence. Let me cite a relevant case in point. Even the great and renowned Indian spinners (such as Bishen Singh Bedi and B.S. Chandrashekhar) did not particularly relish their tour of Pakistan in 1978. In fact, Zaheer Abbas (an elegant stroke player) and Javed Miandad (a forceful striker) virtually finished off the careers of the Indian spinners by plundering runs at will against them. Another hard hitting batsman, Imran Khan, employed similar aggressive tactics to destroy Bedi's bowling at Karachi.

I have always contended that if you play a spinner from the crease (i.e., from a stationary position), the latter can put you under a lot of pressure. Consequently, you would be better advised to use your feet adroitly.

BACK FOOT STROKES

Having dealt with front foot play in a fairly detailed manner, let me now move on to another important aspect of batting, namely, *back foot play*. I consider a batsman to be complete only if he can play equally fluently off both the front foot and the back foot. A really competent batsman must be very quick on his feet and must possess a sharp perception in order to decide almost instantaneously whether to play a particular delivery off the front foot or the back foot. A batsman should *not* commit himself (to either the front or back foot) before the delivery is actually bowled. Although all good batsmen do have a little initial movement, they do not prejudge a delivery before the ball leaves the bowler's hands, i.e., they do not commit themselves. For instance, Viv Richards used to go a bit forward initially, but, at the same time, allowed himself enough leeway to play off the back foot, if so required. A batsman should concentrate on picking the *line* of the ball while facing a fast bowler and on picking the *flight* while facing a spinner. He should not expect juicy half volleys which can easily be despatched to the ropes; instead he should play each delivery on its individual merit.

While facing a battery of menacing pacemen (say, Garner, Holding, Marshall, Lillee, Thomson and Roberts), a batsman perforce tends to play off the back foot (because the delivery invariably tends to be short) for both defensive and aggressive strokes.

While playing a stroke off the back foot, this foot should remain parallel to the batting crease during the initial moments. This stroke should be played close to the body. Obviously, one requires a lot of serious practice and perseverance before one can execute a stroke off the back foot with confidence and precision, be it a defensive one or an attacking one.

Figure 3.10 illustrates different types of back foot strokes.

The Back Foot Defensive Strokes
While playing a back foot defensive stroke, the following points should be kept in mind:

1. Such a stroke is normally played to a short pitched or short of a length delivery, which the batsman cannot force off the back foot because he does not get enough time to hit the ball. Such a delivery is pitched on or outside the off stump.
2. The front (left) shoulder should move just inside the line of the ball with the head forward, leading to a properly balanced body.
3. The back foot should move backward in the line of the delivery.
4. The batsman should stay on his toes to counter both low and high bounce. The body weight should rest on the toes of the right foot, with the left foot positioned near the right foot.
5. In this case, the batsman does not require a high back lift. In fact, the bat should come straight down in the line of the ball with the top (left) hand in full control of the stroke.
6. At the moment of contact between the ball and the bat, the top (left) hand takes control of the stroke and the bottom (right) hand grips the handle (at a lower spot) with the thumb and first finger. The right elbow should touch the body and the left elbow should stay high. The bat should be held vertical (straight).
7. The head should be held down, with the eyes focussed on the ball, looking over or around the handle of the bat.
8. The bat should be close to the inside of the right thigh or should be between the legs. The handle should be angled forward so as to keep the ball down. If the ball

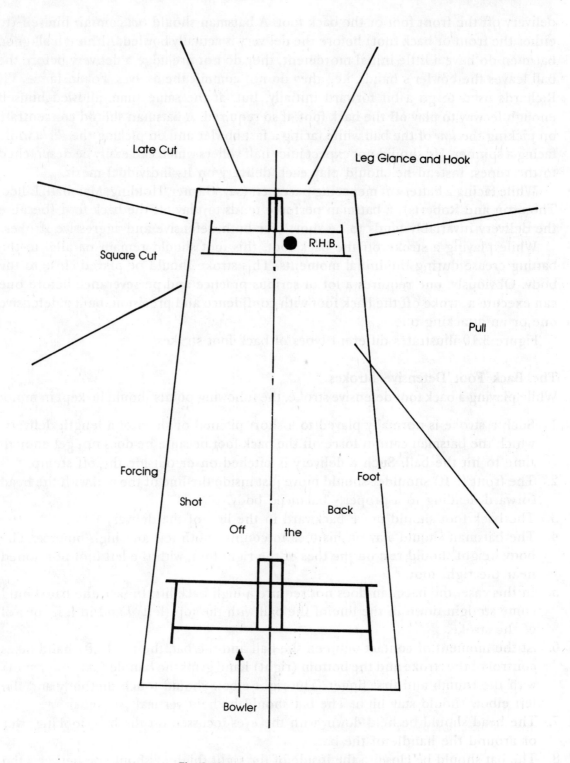

Fig. 3.10 A variety of back foot strokes

happens to bounce high, the left hand should be taken as high as possible and the bat should be completely controlled by just this hand.

9. For playing on the on side, the left shoulder should be open so as to be in line with the delivery. Also, the left hip can be suitably positioned so as to play the shot comfortably.

The Back Foot Push

The back foot push is also sometimes known as the 'bread and butter' stroke. This stroke is played late, with the batsman carefully watching the ball till the last moment before actually middling it. This is a relatively safe stroke and involves less risk. The back foot push proves to be ideal on turning wickets or on those wickets which assist the swing and seam bowlers. This stroke is normally played to a short of a length delivery. The advantage of playing this stroke is that the batsman can give more allowance to the ball and can get more time to play it.

Checklist

1. For this stroke, the batsman requires a high back lift compared to the back foot defensive stroke because he has to force the ball in order to score runs. The batsman may not be able to smash the ball with this stroke but can, nevertheless, utilise it effectively to notch up runs.

2. The batsman's left shoulder and right foot move along the line of the ball, with the head leaning forward.

3. The batsman's right foot should move back and should be parallel to the crease so as to maintain the side-on position.

4. The body weight should rest on the ball of the right foot. The point of contact between the bat and the ball should be close to the body (as long as it can be hit easily).

5. The bat should be brought straight down in the line of the ball and the swing should finish at a high point.

6. As always, the eyes should be kept focussed constantly on the ball.

The English batsman Geoff Boycott was a master of the back foot push and managed to score a lot of runs using this stroke. This stroke is ideal against fast bowlers as it is played close to the body.

The Back Foot Drive

The back foot drive, when perfected against the fast bowlers, makes the batsman emerge a clear winner and provides a lot of delight to the crowds. However, if wrongly executed without getting into the proper position, this stroke can prove disastrous (see Fig. 3.11).

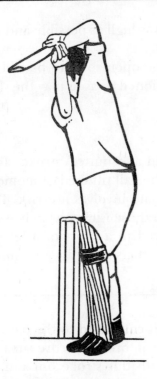

Fig. 3.11   The back foot drive

The West Indian batsmen are superb players of the back foot drive, especially the 3 Ws (Weeks, Worrell and Wallcott), Garfield Sobers, Rohan Kanhai, Clive Lloyd and Viv Richards. Players from other countries too have achieved proficiency in executing this stroke, the prominent ones being the Chappell Brothers, Polly Umrigar, Vijay Manjrekar, Zaheer Abbas, Asif Iqbal and Javed Miandad, all of whom have been a treat to watch.

The back foot drive can be played against both pace and spin.

Checklist

1. The back foot drive is normally played to a short delivery; it can also be played to a short of length delivery.
2. The range of this stroke covers a very wide playing area, i.e., from point to mid-on.
3. As the name implies, this stroke is played off the back foot. The batsman requires a high back lift as he has to hit the ball forcefully.
4. While executing this stroke, the shoulder and the back foot should move along the line of the ball. The shoulder plays an important part in the execution of this stroke, and if it is not turned towards the off side along the line of the delivery, then the batsman could get into serious trouble.
5. While playing the back foot drive, the back foot should go back in the line of the delivery. The batsman should make use of his height to the maximum advantage while striking the ball. The body weight should rest on the ball of the back foot, with the back knee slightly flexed. The shot should be executed from a firm base.
6. The batsman should hit the ball as forcefully as possible (after deciding upon the precise direction), and should complete the stroke with a smooth follow through, with both the hands finishing high. The right shoulder should end up under the chin.
7. The batsman should keep his eyes constantly on the ball, with his head down.
8. A batsman must be careful while playing the back foot drive on turning or seam-assisting wickets. In other words, he should go in for this stroke only when absolutely confident.

The Square Cut

The square cut is an ideal stroke for countering both pace and spin on any kind of wicket, provided it is played perfectly and with full control. This stroke proves very effective in tackling pace bowlers (see Fig. 3.12).

The West Indies and Australian players are adept at executing the square cut because of the nature of their wickets. India has not produced many players who could play the square cut with authority against pace bowling, again, because of the nature of the wickets. However, there are a few Indian batsmen who have achieved proficiency. For instance, Vijay Manjrekar played this stroke with perfection. During my playing days, the square cut perfectionists included G.R. Vishwanath and Mansur Ali Khan Pataudi, who could play it with elegance and control. Most Indian batsmen are capable of executing the square cut against spin bowling; it is against the quick stuff that they are suspect.

The other successful exponents of the square cut include Sobers, Kanhai, Lloyd, Greenidge, Ian Chappell and Greg Chappell, Doug Walters (Australia), Graham Gooch, Asif Iqbal, Javed Miandad and Salim Malik. I remember watching Walters thrash the West Indian pacemen, including Wesley Hall, in the 1968-69 series. He executed ferocious square cuts. Walters again displayed his prowess against Indian spinners at Madras in 1969.

I have not come across any batsman so far who can play the square cut as powerfully and perfectly as Greenidge. He rarely got out while executing this stroke; in fact, even a mishit would go speeding like rocket!

Personally, I do not consider myself a good square cut player, and I try to avoid this stroke to the extent possible.

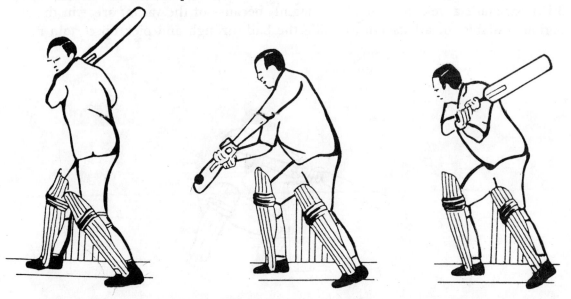

Fig. 3.12   The square cut

Checklist

1. This stroke is played to a short, wide delivery pitched outside the off stump and which bounces at least stump high.
2. The batsman requires a high back lift while playing this stroke, with the front shoulder and the head turned just inside the line of the ball.
3. The back foot should move back and across in the direction of the ball. The body weight rests completely on the back foot, with the knee flexed.
4. The batsman should make contact with the ball in the straight line of the nose, with a full arm stretch, keeping the bat horizontal. The bottom (right) hand should control the stroke; the wrist should be rolled sufficiently to keep the ball down.
5. The right shoulder ends up under the chin, allowing a good follow through of the arms. The bat should finish above the left shoulder.
6. If played properly, this stroke directs the ball between gully and point.
7. A lot of players tend to draw back to play the square cut, which proves dangerous against both pace and spin. In fact, a batsman should lean into the stroke and project his body weight forward when playing. This stroke should not be played to the incoming delivery (pace or spin) as the batsman can get out by playing on, while wielding the bat against the swing or spin.

The Late Cut

Thanks to one-day cricket, the old-fashioned but elegant and attractive *late cut* (Fig. 3.13) has made a welcome comeback, mainly because of the vacant areas in the slip region available for a batsman to guide the ball through and pick up certain runs.

Fig. 3.13 The late cut

Checklist

1. This stroke is played to a short of length delivery which is pitched wide of the off stump and does not bounce very high. A batsman should not attempt the late cut if he is hemmed in by several fielders in the slips and gully. Moreover, he should go in for this stroke only after becoming well set. This stroke is generally played between the first slip and gully.
2. While playing the late cut, the back foot should move back and across the line of the delivery. A high back lift is needed. The batsman should begin this stroke in a manner similar to the square cut. However, instead of smashing the ball, it has to be gracefully guided in the required direction (i.e., between slips and gully).
3. The batsman should play (and control) the stroke with his wrists, keeping his eyes focussed on the ball with his head bent forward. The back is bent as also the right knee. The ball should be hit fractionally late, by the middle of the bat, which is brought down towards the ground.

The late cut was a favourite stroke of G.R. Vishwanath. While executing this stroke, Vishwanath presented an impressive picture of poise and grace.

The Sweep

The sweep (Fig. 3. 14) can be played on any kind of wicket, and serves as an ideal stroke to counter all varieties of spin on a turning wicket. Many batsmen, when they

Fig. 3.14 The sweep

get bogged down, resort to the sweep stroke to get runs. Nevertheless, the sweep can prove useful on certain occasions. I recollect how Graham Gooch went in for the sweep, successfully at that, against the Indian spinners in the 1987 World Cup semifinals. He practically destroyed the Indian spin attack with this one stroke. Much earlier, in 1976, Chandrashekhar and other spinners had effectively used their disguised spin bowling to pester the English batsmen, who eventually, resorted to the sweep, and rather successfully at that, to upset the bowlers' line and length.

The sweep is played to a good length delivery which is pitched in the line of the stumps or outside the leg stump. If played to a straight ball, the batsman could land up in trouble, if he misses the ball.

The sweep was a characteristic shot played by the former England wicket-keeper Alan Knott. In fact, it had become Knott's second nature to go in for the sweep whether the opportunity existed or not. The other renowned batsmen, who could play the sweep adeptly, include Border, Greenidge, Kalicharan, Miandad, Vishwanath and Botham.

Checklist
1. To play the sweep shot, the batsman requires a high back lift. The ball should be hit immediately after it pitches. The batsman should use the 'full arm stretch' action.
2. The front (left) leg should be fully bent (at the knee), allowing the back leg to trail. The shot can be directed towards square leg or fine leg, depending on the angle of the delivery.
3. The batsman should keep his head down, with the eyes watching the ball carefully. The bat, controlled by the right hand, should be brought down sideways, in order to hit the ball forcefully. The point of contact should be somewhere outside the left foot so that even if there is no contact, the ball would hit the pads (and not the wicket).
4. The batsman should lean forward while playing this stroke, with both arms fully stretched.

The Pull

The most effective way of tackling pace is to resort to at least one of the following three strokes: *cut, pull* or *hook.* A batsman who can execute all three strokes competently with a normal technique can dictate terms. Not all batsmen can execute these strokes properly, with the result that they run into difficulties against pace bowling. A batting team can manage without the pull on slow wickets where the ball tends to keep low. But on a fast wicket aiding bounce, one has to be prepared to play the pull shot to effectively counter the short deliveries, and also to score runs.

The pull (Fig. 3.15) is one stroke which one should begin playing at a young age and gradually develop perfection. One must get the basics right in order to play this stroke effectively. One must be able to pinpoint those deliveries which can be pulled;

Fig 3.15 The pull

otherwise, if one picks the wrong ball, one gets either hurt or out.

During the 1983 series in the West Indies, I used the pull to full advantage against the fast bowlers. Another batsman who could play the pull shot with total authority and control was Ian Chappell. Graham Gooch and Alan Border have also utilised the pull to great effect.

Checklist

1. One can play the pull shot only to a delivery which is short and does not bounce more than chest high.

2. This shot is played to a ball that pitches on or just outside the off stump.

3. The pull should be played only to a delivery coming in to the batsman. If a batsman tries to pull against the spin or swing (the outgoing delivery), he may edge the ball to a fielder for a catch.

4. A high back lift is required for the pull and the bat should be swung from wide off the slips or gully.

5. The right foot should go across, the left shoulder should open up and the ball should be taken at a full arm stretch. Only then can the batsman hit the ball down and control the stroke with the right hand. The right foot pivots and when the stroke is completed, the body weight is transferred from the right foot to the left foot.

6. The body balance should be directed forward (to the extent possible) in order to control the shot properly. This stroke is usually played on the leg side in front of the wicket.

7. The batsman should keep his head down, with the eyes constantly focussed on the ball.

8. To play the pull stroke effectively, a batsman must possess an in-built ability to accurately judge the pace and trajectory of the ball and also lightning-quick reflexes and highly agile footwork. The batsman should attempt to lift the ball over the heads of the fielders only if they are standing in close catching positions (or inside the circle in one-day matches). For this stroke, the ball should be taken close to the body, and the batsman should lean back fractionally.

Some of the common mistakes made by batsmen while playing the pull stroke are as follows:

1. They tend to pick the wrong delivery and, hence, land up in trouble.
2. They try to pull a delivery which is too wide off the off stump.
3. They attempt to pull a ball which bounces more than chest high.
4. They tend to play an outgoing delivery or play against the spin, thereby offering a catch.
5. They play the stroke without ascertaining the pace and the bounce of the wicket.
6. They do not take their right foot across; they do not pivot on this foot properly; and they do not shift the body weight on to the left foot properly after the stroke.
7. They have a tendency to keep their heads high in the air, without keeping track (with their eyes) of the ball's trajectory.

An aspiring batsman can master the pull stroke by using a rubber or tennis ball for practice.

The Hook

The most effective way to neutralise a fast bowler's vicious weapon — the bouncer — is to play the hook shot (Fig. 3.16). If a batsman can manage to score some boundaries with this shot, such a move could upset the pace bowler's rhythm and line and could demoralise him. However, a high degree of skill and proficiency is required for playing the hook stroke. I have not come across very many Indian batsmen who could play this stroke properly. The late Vijay Manjrekar was one batsman who could execute this stroke with authority and élan. Sunil Gavaskar used to play the hook stroke initially but gave it up later on. In this context, may I state, without sounding presumptuous, that the hook has come to be associated with my name; in fact, it is my favourite stroke. Several West Indian and Australian batsmen could master the hook stroke because the hard and bouncy wickets provided the ideal stimulus. The all-time greats who could play the hook shot in a commanding manner include Sir Donald Bradman, Sir Garfield Sobers, Rohan Kanhai, Clive Lloyd, Vivian Richards, Gordon Greenidge, and Graham Gooch. Ian Chappell was an excellent improviser of this stroke and used it advantageously to score a lot of runs.

Coming back to my 'hooking' activities, I learnt to play the hook stroke at a very young age, instinctively. I recall playing a fair amount of cricket with tennis and rubber balls during my boyhood. This helped me get used to the high bounce needed to play the hook stroke. My schooling days were in Punjab, and turf wickets were a rarity in those days. Consequently, I used to play on matting wickets, which aided me in effectively tackling the short rising delivery. My father, the legendary Lala Amarnath, also encouraged me to play the hook. Although I had got out a number of times while playing the hook, I did not give it up because I believed that this is a scoring stroke and the ideal tactic for demoralising a pace bowler. I remember the heavy dose of criticism and condemnation that I was subjected to when I was out hit wicket (while attempting the hook) to a delivery from the Australian paceman Rodney Hogg (in 1979). The press, the electronic media, the so-called selectors and even some of my friends concluded that I would never play for India again. Just to prove them wrong, I worked assiduously on improving my technique by going in for a more open stance. As a result, I could execute the hook stroke with a greater degree of control and precision.

A note of caution needs to be sounded regarding the hook stroke. Whenever any batsman intends to play this stroke, he should pick the right delivery with the proper line and adequate bounce. If he

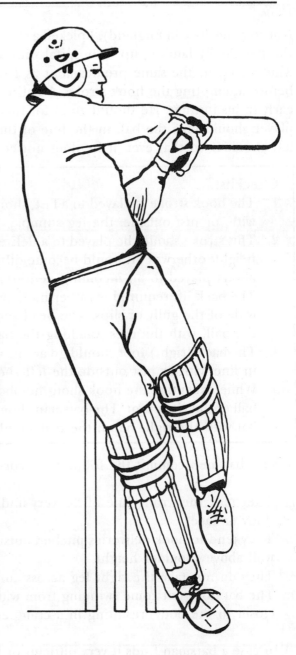

Fig. 3.16   The hook

happens to choose a delivery with a wrong line or with excessively high bounce or if he does not roll his wrists correctly, there is a possibility that the ball would fly into the air after making contact with the bat (at the top edge). Also, in such a situation, the ball might hit the body, causing physical injury. Such an incident occurred in my case when I was facing Sir Richard Hadlee (in 1979, while playing against

Nottinghamshire in England). I picked a wrong line of that particular delivery and paid the penalty by landing up in hospital with a fractured skull. Consequently, to avoid winding up in the same predicament as I did, I sincerely recommend *strict caution* before attempting the hook stroke. A batsman should desist from playing this stroke early in his innings. He should go in for the hook only after getting well settled. The player should take the ball in the line of the left shoulder or slightly away from the left shoulder so that even if he does not connect, the ball sails past the body.

Checklist

1. The hook stroke is played to a fast, short, rising delivery, which pitches in line with, or just outside, the leg stump.
2. This stroke should be played to a delivery which does not rise above shoulder height; otherwise, it would become difficult to control the ball. This stroke is always played to an incoming delivery.
3. The back lift required is rather high and the bat should come swinging from wide of the gully or slips. The head should be positioned outside the line of the ball, with the eyes watching the ball very carefully.
4. The back (right) foot should go across and the batsman should strike the ball in line with or just outside the left shoulder.
5. While executing the hook shot, the body weight should be transferred to the ball of the right foot. The batsman should then pivot his body and control the bat with the right hand; the ball should be kept down.

Several batsmen commit the following errors while attempting to hook:

1. They pick the wrong line of delivery and, consequently, the ball rams into their body or face.
2. They tend to hook deliveries pitched outside the off stump or those which bounce well above shoulder height.
3. They do not take the right leg across correctly.
4. The bat does not come swinging from wide of the gully or slips but is held much closer to the body, resulting in a cramped and uncomfortable position.

In case a batsman finds it very difficult or impractical to play the hook stroke, the best method to avoid it is by ducking. Alternatively, the batsman could just sway away from the delivery. Whatever his decision, he should never take his eyes off the ball.

As should be evident by now, the hook is one of the most difficult strokes to master; but the task is definitely not impossible. Invariably, the ball tends shoot up into the air while playing a hook stroke (i.e., if incorrectly played). However, if a batsman perseveres and practises with grit and determination, he can achieve success, and prove his capabilities.

The Leg Glance

The leg glance is a delicate and graceful stroke. It can be played off both the back foot and the front foot. This stroke is played to a short of a length delivery pitched on, or just outside, the leg stump with both precision and control. The 'perfect practitioners' of the leg glance include Sunil Gavaskar, Geoff Boycott, Javed Miandad and Ravi Shastri.

When playing off the front foot, the leg glance should be attempted in the case of a slightly overpitched delivery on, or just outside, the leg stump. This stroke is mostly played to incoming deliveries.

The Back Foot Leg Glance

As the name suggests, this stroke is played off the back foot on the leg side. The batsman should take his back (right) leg across and drop his left shoulder a bit. The ball should be taken outside the line of the left pad. The bat should come from wide off the slips. The batsman should allow the ball to come close to his body before playing the stroke. This would enable him to control the shot and keep the ball down. The batsman should roll his wrists to the required degree (in an anticlockwise direction) in order to deflect the ball to the leg side. The stroke is controlled by the right hand, keeping the handle of the bat forward. This ensures that the ball is kept down and goes between square leg and fine leg. This stroke should be played as late as possible in order to achieve good control. I have noticed many batsmen tending to totter or fall on the off side while executing this stroke, with the result that they spoon an easy catch to any close-in fielder on the leg side.

I have never seen Sunil Gavaskar getting out while playing the leg glance because he had excellent control over the stroke. He never played this stroke in a hurry or out of impetuosity nor did he try to hit the ball too hard. Many batsmen make the mistake of playing the delivery too early, and away from the body, thereby lofting a catch to a leg slip or a square leg fielder. The ideal manner of playing this stroke is to wait for the ball to come to the bat, with the eyes watching the ball constantly.

The Front Foot Leg Glance

This stroke is played to a slightly overpitched delivery, outside the leg stump. The batsman should avoid playing this stroke too far away from his body because, in such a situation, he might end up offering a catch to a close-in fielder (leg slip or short square leg). The body balance should be kept in control so that the ball can be directed downwards. One should not attempt the front foot leg glance in case a delivery is pitched in the line of the stumps.

Checklist

1. The batsman should start playing the front foot leg glance as if he were playing a forward defence stroke. The bat should come in from wide off the slips.
2. The batsman should drop or open his left shoulder. He should keep the bat vertical and then turn his wrists (in an anticlockwise direction).
3. Before contact is established between the bat and the ball, the batsman's body and head should lean forward. Also, the bat handle should be angled forward. The head should stay down, with the eyes firmly focussed on the ball (this repetition seems unavoidable, but necessary). The batsman should flex his front knee so that he can lean on the front foot while playing the stroke.

A FEW WORTHWHILE TIPS

Batting constitutes a skill that has to be perfected through vigorous practice, careful observation and persistent perseverance. It is no easy task, but sheer grit and determination can lead to proficiency and success. I would like to emphasise here that no one is a master of all aspects of cricket and one must remain a student of the game constantly. One should always be receptive to other people's ideas, views or tips and pick up relevant points to improve one's batting skills.

As mentioned earlier, you can improve your game and hone it to perfection by watching other accomplished batsmen (either on TV or on the field) and learn quite a lot about technique and style. The ideal batsman possesses the following characteristics:

1. He has a comfortable but firm grip; plays side on; is quick on his feet; and manages to gain a fraction of a second more to play his shot compared to run-of-the-mill players.
2. He watches the bowler's hand very carefully and judges the type of ball to be delivered rather early and accordingly plays his stroke.
3. He maintains his composure even under great pressure and never plays a rash or impetuous shot in a hurry. He keeps his head down and his eyes focussed on the ball (pardon the repetition!).

Cricket, in some ways, can be compared to chess. As a batsman, you would have to plan a broad, overall strategy, but depending on the opponents' moves, you have to vary or improvise your on-the-field tactics. You should try and obtain relevant information on the rival team members' strong points and drawbacks and accordingly plan a counterattack. Do not get disheartened or dejected if you cannot play all the strokes perfectly, but, instead, try to concentrate on those strokes about which you are confident.

Many youngsters, on watching other accomplished batsmen play beautiful and seemingly effortless strokes, attempt to blindly imitate their 'idols'. This can prove unfruitful; what is needed is to learn the basic technique and utilise it according to one's capabilities and limitations. Let me illustrate this point with an example. As a kid, I recollect practising with the Indian Railways team, one of whose members was Vijay Mehra, who had just returned from the West Indian tour of 1962. He was highly impressed by Rohan Kanhai's execution of the hook shot. Mehra was one player who could not play this stroke. At the nets, he tried to copy Kanhai's style without really possessing the requisite skill and agility. He paid a rather heavy price; he was hit on the face by a rising delivery and had to be taken to hospital for treatment. Incidentally, he also had a tooth broken on this occasion.

Some players tend to take the net practice sessions rather casually and, consequently, develop certain bad habits, which adversely affect their game, be it batting, bowling, fielding or wicket-keeping. Consequently, when they are actually playing a match, and when a lot of pressure is exerted on them, they are unable to cope with the situation. Therefore, practice sessions must be given due importance and seriousness so that a player can face any challenge while playing a match, especially at the highest levels (international levels).

One topic that is constantly discussed is how to tackle fast bowlers, especially those of world class calibre. Despite the fact that wickets in India are rather slow and the conditions are not conducive to pace bowling, we have produced some outstanding players against fast bowling: for instance, Vijay Hazare, Vijay Manjrekar, Lala Amarnath, Vinoo Mankad, Polly Umrigar, Sunil Gavaskar, G.R. Vishwanath and K. Srikkant. One of the reasons I can think of can be attributed to the tennis ball, which is extremely popular in India, especially among kids. This ball is difficult to play, because it bounces a great deal and comes slowly after pitching. Consequently, a batsman acquires an excellent 'ball sense', i.e., the ability to judge how exactly to play the stroke while keeping the ball down (coping with the bounce).

Another factor relates to matting wickets, which are ideal for practice in tackling pace and bounce, especially off the back foot.

An unorthodox, but useful, way of tackling pace bowling is as follows: At the nets, ask any fast bowler to overstep the crease and bowl from a distance of 20 yards (instead of the normal 22 yards). The ball would thus come quicker, enabling you to quicken your reflexes to cope with the pace.

One problem faced by young players relates to concentration. While playing in a top level match, how can one really concentrate in the midst of so much hustle and bustle and commotion? Here are a few worthwhile tips:

1. Always think of playing one delivery at a time. If you have earlier played a bad shot and have been beaten, forget about it.
2. Different players use different methods to maintain their concentration. For instance, Sunil Gavaskar would not talk at all to the non-striker in the beginning of his innings for fear of losing his concentration. On the contrary, Javed Miandad

loved to chatter away; the more talkative he became, the better was his game. Lawrence Rowe of the West Indies used to whistle every time he played a stroke. Srikkant used to wander around the wicket after every delivery, muttering something to himself. Thus, try to develop your own 'formula' for concentration!

3. You must constantly bear in mind the fact that any bowler cannot bowl more than one ball at a time. Also, do not get overawed by the name or reputation of the bowler. Do not underestimate your own talent or abilities. You must understand that you will be competing on a one-to-one basis. For example, a team may consist of four great fast bowlers, but one only can bowl at a time! Thus, concentrate on each and every delivery!

It would be appropriate to mention in this context the amazing concentration powers of, who else, but Sunil Gavaskar! Gavaskar once told me that he could concentrate on reading a book even if surrounded by 10,000 people! No wonder he could achieve so many distinctions and establish so many records!

RUNNING BETWEEN THE WICKETS

Running between the wickets plays an important role in a batsman's and (by logical extension) the team's chances of achieving victory. The fundamental job of any batsman is to score as many runs as possible. It is not always possible to hit fours and sixes; therefore, the batsman must go in for singles, two's, or three's to keep the scoreboard moving! Consequently, the batsman and the non-striker must have very good understanding and coordination between themselves while batting in the middle.

It is very important for the striker and the non-striker to safeguard each other's wickets while taking runs. It is essential to know precisely how fast your partner can run, and chalk out the strategy accordingly. If there is one slow runner and one fast runner at the wicket, the consequences could be adverse, because of lack of coordination and understanding; one of the batsmen invariably falls victim to run out. I am reminded of former Indian all-rounder, Abid Ali, who was a very fast runner but could not at all coordinate with his partner. Abid Ali must have been responsible for a large number of run outs (either losing his own wicket or getting the non-striker out).

The basic or first activity that a non-striker has to perform is to take a start as soon as the bowler has delivered the ball. This would enable him to reach the other end quickly, if so required. (Here, 'start' means that the non-striker should come down the pitch at least a few yards, and remain on his toes, ready to go for a run if the opportunity arises.)

The non-striker has to stand on the other side of the stumps with respect to the side from which the bowler is operating. In other words, if he is bowling from over the wicket (off side), the non-striker has to stand on the on side. The non-striker should hold the bat at the top with one hand in order to achieve a greater reach if he has to fully stretch himself to regain his crease in case of a close call. The hand in which the bat is to be held would depend on whether the bowler is operating from over the wicket or around the wicket.

A word of caution: The non-striker should not step out of the crease before the bowler has delivered the ball; otherwise he is liable to be stumped by the bowler himself. This is what happened to Peter Kirsten (South Africa), when Kapil Dev got him out (Kirsten was out of his crease) in a test match. The bowler can easily 'run out' a non-striker without delivering the ball, if the latter happens to be standing outside the crease, while taking the start. Therefore, one has to be cautious while going in for the start.

If the non-striker happens to be a runner for an injured batsman, then an increased degree of understanding and coordination becomes essential, especially when the injured batsman is facing the bowler. Such a substitute runner usually stands near the square leg empire, within an imaginary line parallel to the batting crease. The substitute runner should go in for a run only when absolutely sure; otherwise, if he steps out of the crease, and is stumped, the main batsman would be declared out.

A *call* is essential for both the striker and the non-striker. Usually, the player facing the ball (as opposed to the player who has his back to the ball) should give the call. It should be a resounding and unambiguous *yes* or *no*, so as to avoid any mix-up. In case the call is positive, the players should sprint across quickly and reach the opposite sides as swiftly as possible. In the process, they should take care not to bump into each other or collide with any fielder. Normally, when the batsman (striker) plays a stroke behind the wicket, it becomes the non-striker's duty to give the call (either yes or no), because the striker may not be in a position to look backwards and then make a decision. On the other hand, for any stroke played behind the non-striker (mid-off, mid-on, long off, long on), it becomes the striker's duty to give the call.

Let us now discuss the common mistakes that batsmen make while running between the wickets. Sometimes, the non-striker, when the ball is behind him, instead of looking at the striker for the call, turns around to locate the ball, thus delaying him and also causing confusion because the striker might have responded with a 'no', whereas the non-striker might still be running towards the danger end! Another mistake commonly made is that the call is not loud enough to be heard.

If there is a possibility of an extra run, even as the striker and non-striker cross each other, they can decide whether to go in for that run or not by shouting clearly.

Quick singles always involve some degree of risk, especially if you play a ball defensively and want to steal a run. Or else, if you want to take a chance and go in for an extra run, you should stretch yourself fully, even diving if necessary, at the last moment, to regain the crease, without fear of getting hurt. One should be confident and aggressive while batting and make the utmost efforts to complete the run(s). Nothing could be more frustrating or depressing than getting run out, which I consider a sheer waste. One has to be very careful, but at the same time, positive, while running between the wickets.

Whenever you play a stroke and intend going for runs you must complete your first run as fast as possible, especially if the ball has travelled to a deep position such as deep third man, deep fine leg or deep point. This puts extra pressure on the fielders; as a result, they tend to misfield or fumble with the ball, affording an opportunity to go in for an extra run.

Javed Miandad stands out an excellent sprinter between the wickets. He has the uncanny ability (of course, along with his partner) to convert singles into two's and two's into three's!

In one-day cricket, where just a few runs could make all the difference between victory and defeat, running between the wickets becomes a crucially important factor.

Whenever you play a stroke, whether on the off side or the on side, in front of the wickets, make sure that your eyes follow the trajectory of the ball. Assuming that you have played a shot on the off side to a fairly deep position and you intend taking two or three runs, the following points should be borne in mind by both the striker and the non-striker:

1. While completing the first run and when about to turn for beginning the second run, you should touch the crease at the non-striker's end with the bat held in the left hand so that you can keep your eyes on the ball and also on the fielders. Next, while about to complete the second run and turn back for the third run, touch the crease at the batsman's end with the bat held in the right hand. (This sequence applies to additional runs, if intended to be taken.)
2. The non-striker should also keep his eyes on the ball whenever he is in a position to do so. He should touch the crease with the bat held in the right hand when turning for the second run and while turning for the third run, he should touch the crease with the bat held in the left hand. (This sequence applies to additional runs, if intended to be taken.) One should remember that a run is completed only when both the batsman and the non-striker have regained their respective creases.

Some batsmen, either due to inexperience or due to recklessness, tend to botch up while running between the wickets, even at the higher levels of cricket. For instance, I have observed players going for the second and third runs, not really bothering to keep their eyes on the ball and while having their backs to the fielder. Sometimes, they do not respond to their partner's call until it is too late. Inevitably, they wind up as run out victims.

A batsman should be able to judge the capabilities and weaknesses of the individual fielders. To the extent possible, he should direct his strokes towards the relatively less agile and less nimble footed fielders so that he can gain maximum advantage. Another important factor to be borne in mind is that a batsman should know whether a particular fielder is left handed or right handed. For instance, if a fielder is left handed, then by playing a stroke to his right, a batsman can safely go in for quick runs, because the fielder cannot pick up and throw the ball immediately. However, one has to be very careful when playing a stroke to a fielder who is ambidextrous (i.e., who can use both hands equally well).

Running between the wickets involves a high degree of skill and proficiency and requires a lot of thinking and planning. Sensible batsmen would adapt their game according to the field placement and bowling potential.

Let us now take up some specific situations. If the fielders are stationed at deep positions (such as long on, long off, deep square leg or deep mid-on), then the intelligent batsman would just tap the ball close to the wicket and dart across for a quick single, instead of trying to hit or push the ball forcefully towards the boundary. On the other hand, when the fielders are stationed close to the bat, the ideal tactic would be to hit powerfully so as to score runs (boundaries, three's or two's). Of course, theoretically, it is very easy to give advice or instructions, but practically they are difficult to execute unless one has the requisite aptitude, skill, experience and the right frame of mind.

I have come across a large number of batsmen who have fallen victims to run out due to a misfield because of hesitation. By the time a batsman recovers his presence of mind and decides to go for the run, it is too late. There is a 'golden rule' in cricket stating 'never run on a misfield', provided the ball is within the fielder's reach.

Some seemingly obvious, but often neglected, facts need to be reiterated. A batsman finds it easier to set off for a run after playing a stroke off the front foot, because he would already be ahead of the crease and would have less distance to cover. On the contrary, when a batsman plays a stroke off the back foot, he is at a disadvantage because he has moved back a yard or so, and thus has to cover additional ground. Therefore, an extra bit of alacrity is needed to complete the run because the player's body weight would be resting on the back foot and he requires additional precious time to recover his balance, get into gear and then begin running. One may think a yard or so may not be all that difficult to cover but, at times, that gap could prove crucial. So, the batsman should attempt a run only when he is absolutely sure of reaching the other end well within time.

Whenever a batsman comes under tremendous pressure and is in a great rush to reach the safety of the crease, he would find it useful to drag his bat on the ground (for the last few yards) rather than flailing it in the air. This could prove life-saving at times, as the precious few seconds saved could make all the difference.

On setting off for a run, a batsman should hold the bat with both hands; one hand holding the handle and the other the blade, so that it does not slip out of his hand, or get entangled between his legs. (This is what happened to Srikkant in the one-day international against Pakistan at Calcutta in 1989. As a result, he fell on to the wicket and was run out.) Of course, as you near the crease, you should hold the bat with only one hand either left or right, depending on the convenience.

From the foregoing discussion, it is obvious that running between the wickets forms an essential, if not crucial, aspect of the game.

Four
The Fielding Department

Ever since one-day cricket has begun to dominate the international arena, the standard of fielding has perforce improved immensely due to the fiercely competitive nature of the sport. Fielders have become more conscious of their role and have been infused with new confidence and also aggressiveness. Their levels of physical fitness have also improved considerably in order to meet the tremendous demands of the game with respect to mobility, agility and reflexes.

Nowadays, we come across 'specialist fielders', i.e., fielders who specialise in particular positions (say, slips, covers, mid-wicket or point). (The various fielding positions are illustrated in Fig. 4.1.) During my childhood days, I can recollect only two specialist fielders, namely, Colin Bland and Bobby Simpson. The former was an outstanding outfield specialist and the latter stood out for his performance in the slips.

In the olden days, not much attention was paid to the fielding department. When I played my first test against Australia in 1969, I cannot recall going through any rigorous fielding sessions. The players used to come over to the ground, practise batting and bowling for a while and pack up. (It was only some years later that the importance of fielding came to be fully realised.) Although we had some competent close-in fielders at that time, it was Eknath Solkar who stood out as unique among them. His reflexes, ball sense and powers of concentration were truly amazing, and he took some incredible catches during his time. In fact, he had the potential to turn a losing match into a winning proposition by his spectacular fielding. When the Indian touring team beat England (in the 1971 series) it was Solkar's phenomenal fielding performance which was instrumental in India's victory. One should remember that helmets were not in vogue at that time. It would not be an exaggeration to claim that top-class fielders can turn an ordinary bowling side into a good bowling side and a good bowling side into a match-winning side.

I think it was Bobby Simpson (former Australian captain) who aptly remarked that "catches win matches". A professional fielding side should practise a great deal before a match or series, and, during the actual game, exert a lot of pressure on the batsmen,

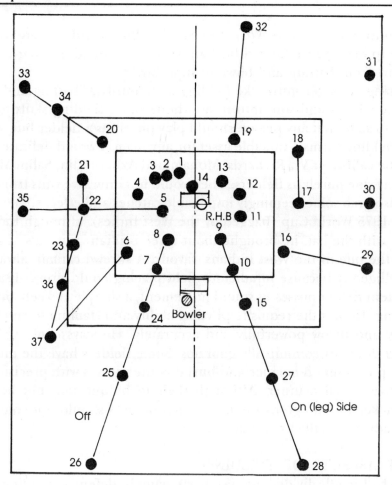

Close Field	In Field	Out Field
1. First Slip	15. Mid-on	25. Deep Mid-off
2. Second Slip	16. Mid-wicket	26. Long Off
3. Third Slip	17. Square-leg	27. Deep Mid-on
4. Gully	18. Backward Square Leg	28. Long-on
5. Silly Point	19. Short Fine Leg	29. Deep Mid-wicket
6. Short Extra	20. Short Third Man	30. Deep Square Leg
7. Short Mid-off	21. Backward Point	31. Long Leg
8. Silly Mid-off	22. Point	32. Deep Fine Leg
9. Silly Mid-on	23. Cover Point	33. Deep Third Man
10. Short Mid-on	24. Mid-off	34. Third Man
11. Forward Short Leg		35. Deep Point
12. Backward Short Leg		36. Extra-cover
13. Leg Slip		37. Deep Extra
14. Wicket-Keeper		

Fig. 4.1 The various fielding positions

forcing them to commit errors. We could bag the 1983 World Cup and the 1985 World Championship because we fielded brilliantly in the outfield and hardly dropped any catches, apart from batting and bowling superbly.

Any aspiring cricketer must take fielding as seriously as batting and bowling. One must put one's heart and soul into it, and hone one's fielding skills to perfection. I don't mean to state that any person should play purely as a fielder but one should not forget that fielding forms a valuable asset for any team. I would definitely love to have fielders of the calibre of Viv Richards, Mohammed Azharuddin, Salim Malik and Jonty Rhodes on my side purely as fielders. They would not only save runs from being scored but would also grab some seemingly impossible catches and effect some incredible run outs. In the 1975 World Cup (bagged by the West Indies), although Richards did not do very well with the bat, he brought about three brilliant run outs at a crucial stage and turned the tide in the West Indians' favour. A shrewd captain always deploys his fielders intelligently because injudicious field placing could prove disastrous.

A competent fielder possesses sound judgement, a sharp eye, keen anticipation and perfect timing. He has the requisite physical ability and stamina to run very fast, pick up smoothly and throw powerfully and accurately. He stays cool even under great pressure and does not commit silly goof-ups. Some fielders have the inborn ability to chase a ball, pick it up off balance and hurl it at the wickets with precision, sometimes in an unconventional manner. Although their technique may not be approved by orthodox cricketers, who go by the book, such fielders should not change their style as this may adversely affect their performance.

DIFFERENT ASPECTS OF FIELDING

Fielding can be broadly divided into two parts, namely, defensive fielding and attacking fielding (intercepting and retrieving). In defensive fielding, the player merely stops the ball, whereas, in attacking fielding, the player charges towards (or after) the ball, retrieves it and tries to get a batsman run out by shying at the wickets (or to the wicket-keeper or bowler, depending on the specific situation).

Defensive Fielding

Defensive type of fielding can be resorted to once a fielder is sure that there is no opportunity to get a batsman run out or there is no possibility of the batsmen going for a run (or an extra run as the case may be).

There are two chief methods (see Fig. 4.2) of stopping the ball (after the batsman has played a stroke) which are effective on different types of grounds.

The first method involves stopping the ball by both the hands in front of the right ankle by stooping accordingly. This method is useful if the field is lush and green and has an even bounce and where the ball rolls smoothly along the ground.

The second method, called the 'long barrier', is applicable in the case of an uneven field, which may contain tiny stones, small holes, and which is very dry (like many fields in India). This method involves going down on one knee (left) and appropriately bending the other, and stopping the ball near the left knee with both hands.

Let me describe both methods in a little more detail.

In the first method, the fielder should, first of all, position himself correctly to intercept the ball. When the ball comes towards him, he bends his right knee a little, with the head down and the

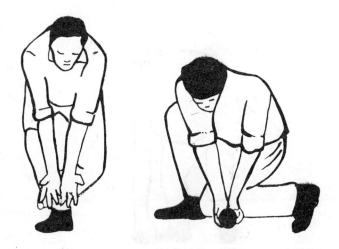

Fig. 4.2 The two chief defensive fielding techniques

eyes on the ball. The fielder bends his back (stoops a bit) so that his hands can reach the ball. The ball is caught by the hands in front of the right ankle. The palms should be kept open so as to allow the ball to come into them. The most important factor is taking up the exact position, after anticipating the speed and direction of the ball. If one misjudges these factors, one could get hurt, if the batsman's shot is a powerful one.

The second method (or the long barrier) is more effective and safer. After judging the trajectory and the pace of the ball after the shot, the fielder moves into the line of the ball. The right ankle is positioned behind the line of the ball, with the left knee bent fully on the ground in front of the right heel to make sure there is no gap anywhere. This position offers a 'long barrier' defence. The eyes should watch the ball carefully and then the hands should be so positioned close together to catch the ball, with the fingers pointing down, touching the ground. From this position the fielder can move quickly into a throwing position, if required.

Attacking Fielding

Attacking fielding is usually done close to the wicket, when a fielder virtually pounces on the ball, picks it up and flings it at the wicket, all in one motion, to get a batsman run out.

One-day cricket, which proves much more exciting and action packed than the traditional three-day or five-day matches, provides an ideal opportunity for attacking fielding. For instance, when the batsmen go in for a quick run, the fielder darts towards the ball and tries to run out one of the batsmen. In this context, the following points are noteworthy:

1. The fielder should always keep his eyes on the ball. He should ideally intercept the ball outside his right foot (Fig. 4.3). He should bend his front knee a little so

that he can also bend his back and the right hand can reach the ball easily. Once the ball is in the right hand, this arm (right) should be swung back (to prepare for the throw) to the required extent (i.e., depending on the distance from the wicket) and then released forward, with a flick of the wrist to eject the ball with force, keeping the eyes on the target. The throw can be along the ground or in the air, aimed straight at the wickets. The body weight should be properly balanced in order to achieve maximum effect. (An underarm throw can be resorted to if the situation warrants it.) (See Fig. 4.4.)

Fig. 4.3 Intercepting the ball (outside the right foot)

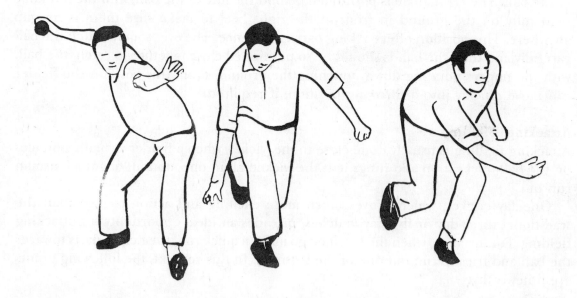

Fig. 4.4 Different throwing styles

2. I have come across many players who field exceptionally well throughout the game, but when they get a run out opportunity, they botch it up, mainly because they take their eyes off the ball. Instead of concentrating on the ball, they tend to look at the batsman, thus compelling them to pick up the ball in great hurry. As a result, they fumble with the ball or miss it completely. Thus, it is important to stay cool and concentrate on the ball. Once the player has got the ball in his hands, he can aim for the wickets.

3. For long distance fielding, the player should pick up the ball with both hands; he should maintain a sideways position, so that he can throw it easily and powerfully. While fielding in the deep position, the ball can come on any side of the body. Consequently, the fielder should be able to anticipate the trajectory of the ball immediately after the batsman has played the stroke. After that, the player should not merely wait for the ball to reach him, but should charge towards the ball so as to intercept it en route and thus exert pressure on the batsman. The fielder should take the ball in the line of his right ankle, but should pick it up inside his left foot, with both hands, while maintaining a face-on position (*vis-à-vis* the ball) throughout the period of action. Next, the fielder should position himself such that his right foot comes behind the left foot. The right arm should be stretched back fully, with the left hand providing the precise counterpoise. The eyes should be focussed on the target and then the fielder should eject the ball with maximum force (Fig.4.5).

Fig. 4.5 The method for the long throw

There are two other methods used for long throws. The first is when a fielder is chasing a slow moving ball. Instead of picking it up outside the right foot, the fielder can do so inside of his left foot, then turn and throw the ball accurately towards the target, all in one smooth action.

The second method pertains to a ball which has stopped in the deep field. In this case, the fielder should charge a bit ahead of the ball, turn around, pick up the ball inside of the left foot and throw it with a smooth action towards the target. When picking up the ball, the fielder should ensure that his eyes are focussed on it and his head is kept down.

THE IMPORTANCE OF THE THROW

It's very important for every fielder to have a good throw, which should be both accurate and timely. A fielder may prove to be brilliant in catching and stopping the ball, by moving with the speed of a cheetah, but if his throw is not accurate, all efforts would be wasted. All successful fielders must possess good throwing abilities. In fact, it is a treat to watch in action superb fielders such as Viv Richards, Mohammed Azharuddin, David Gower, Robin Smith, Salim Malik, Jonty Rhodes and Roger Harper. All of them can move swiftly and throw accurately. Moreover, the crowds love to witness a display of brilliant fielding and throwing especially if a spectacular run out is achieved!

As already mentioned, accuracy is the hallmark of a good throw. Each throw should be fully backed, especially at the bowler's end, where the ball should be collected behind the wickets so that a stumping can be effected either by removing the bails or by breaking the wicket. Even at the wicket-keeper's end, the throw must be backed by the nearest fielder. There is nothing more frustrating than the fielding side giving away runs as a result of bad throwing and faulty back-up, especially in a one-day match, where every run is precious.

While throwing, a fielder should maintain a side-on position. For long-distance throwing, the throwing arm should be taken back fully, with the other arm pointing in the direction of the throw. The body weight should initially rest on the right leg, and while actually throwing, the player should pivot on to the left foot (so as to gain the required momentum). He should effectively utilise various parts of the body, such as wrists, shoulder, elbow, arm and torso in order to achieve maximum impact. Needless to say, the eyes should constantly be focussed on the target.

Another vital factor during throwing is the *grip*. If the grip is not correct, brilliant fielding and a strong arm shall come to nought. As soon as the fielder has transferred the ball to this throwing hand, his first two fingers should come on top of the ball with the thumb underneath (like a pace bowler's grip) or else, the first two fingers should be placed across the seam, with the thumb underneath. However, one should not waste time looking for the seam; in fact, one should automatically grip the ball correctly as soon as one picks it up. For long distances, the fielder should take his hand back and hurl the ball powerfully using the various parts of the body to the maximum effect, as described earlier. If a player holds the ball in his palm, he would not be able to throw it far nor accurately.

CATCHING SKILLS

Catching is a crucial factor in the game of cricket. In fact, a team's success or failure depends on its catching abilities. At times, a single catch can determine the fate of a match. I remember watching (on TV) an India-Pakistan match played at Sharjah. The Indians were chasing a stiff target, but were moving smoothly towards achieving it. Sachin Tendulkar was going great guns. He had lofted Salim Malik for two glorious sixes, and made a third attempt to score a six. Unfortunately, the ball did not soar beyond the ropes and the agile Pakistani fielder Mushtaq Ahmed, positioned at deep mid-wicket, ran about 20 yards and then dived forward to pick up a brilliant tumbling catch, which changed the course of the game. (India ultimately lost the match.) Another instance that comes to my mind is when India beat Pakistan (in 1985) in a low scoring match. Sunil Gavaskar snapped up several brilliant catches in the slips, which turned the tables in India's favour. Also, who can forget Kapil Dev's magnificent catch to dismiss Viv Richards at a crucial stage of the game during the 1983 World Cup?

Regardless of a fielder's position, just one vital catch held by him can boost the morale of the entire team. On the contrary, a dropped catch can produce the opposite effect, i.e., demoralising the entire team. For example, when India was playing against the West Indies at Bridgetown, Barbados, in 1983, Gus Logie, a newcomer, was struggling to establish his place in the Windies team. He had hardly scored any runs, when S. Venkataraghavan dropped a simple catch (in the slips) lobbed from Logie's gloves. Logie then went on to score a century, which helped West Indies beat India quite convincingly. Similarly, in the 1976 India vs. West Indies match at Trinidad, Clive Lloyd miscued an on-drive, with the result that the ball shot up into the air between mid-off and covers, in between two fielders. Each fielder thought that the other would take the catch and both stayed put. Had that catch been taken, India could have defeated the Windies easily. The foregoing examples clearly underscore the importance of catches in determining the course of a match.

Everyone admires a fielder who makes sincere efforts to take a catch, howsoever difficult it may seem. Such efforts not only give him satisfaction but the crowds also enjoy the spectacle. It is a pleasure to watch fielders such as Viv Richards, Dean Jones, Azharuddin, Salim Malik, Jonty Rhodes and Roger Harper in action. They make fielding look so simple. I am a strong believer in the maxim that nothing is impossible provided one is willing to put in hard work and perseverance. Here are a few basics a fielder has to keep in mind while attempting catches:

1. He should concentrate on each and every ball, assuming a catch would come his way.
2. He should keep his head still and begin moving only after clearly sighting the ball.
3. He must have a good body balance and should remain constantly alert.
4. His hand should be in a relaxed position, with the palms facing outwards.
5. He should keep his arms slightly flexed so that he can adjust his hands accordingly in order to catch the ball comfortably.

Catching can be divided into two broad categories: (1) Close-in catching(Fig. 4.6) and (2) outfield catching. (The aforementioned basics apply to both categories.) Let us now discuss each category individually.

Fig. 4.6 Close-in catching

Close-in fielding plays a very important role in the initial stages of an innings, especially when pace bowlers are operating. I still recall one particular match between England and Australia at Leeds in the 1980-81 series. England defeated Australia despite being forced to follow on as a result of their inspiring and amazing close-in catching.

Close-in catches can pop up anywhere near the wicket. The usual positions are slips, gully, silly point, silly mid-off, silly mid-on, forward short leg, short square leg and leg slip.

You must have noticed different fielders adopting different stances. Some stand with their hands resting on their knees and some others follow the traditional style, i.e., legs apart and hands in front. I personally prefer the old-fashioned stance, whose essentials are as follows:

1. The fielder should take up a crouching position. The distance between the spread out feet should be such that the stance proves comfortable (shoulder width is the right distance).
2. The hands should be in front with the palms facing outwards and slightly cupped. The eyes should be on the ball.
3. The fielder should always be ready to go for the catch, even if he were to drop it. I would prefer a fielder who attempts a catch, rather than a fielder who doesn't try at all.
4. The fielders should maintain a safe distance between them in a close-in position. The slips area usually contains more number of fielders. A safe method of keeping

the right distance is to stretch one's arms to one's sides and just touch the fingers of the fielders on either side (if so positioned).

5. The fielder should maintain his concentration constantly and should go for the catches with both hands. If not possible, only then should he attempt one-handed catches.

6. The body weight should be equally balanced on the balls of both feet so that the fielder can move quickly if required.

7. The eyes should be on the same level and the head should be absolutely still and relaxed.

The close-in positions with respect to a batsman are now described.

Slips

The best catchers normally specialise in the slips. Such fielders have quick reflexes, good anticipation and a great deal of concentration. When pace bowlers are operating, most of the catches come to the slips. A slip fielder should begin moving only after catching sight of the ball and making sure that the ball is coming his way and not going to another slip fielder stationed nearby. In other words, one slip fielder should not intrude upon another slip fielder's territory, because such an intrusion could result in a clash. Thus, the slip fielders should maintain a safe distance between themselves and should have extremely quick coordination. One slip should stand slightly ahead of the other to avoid collisions. Normally, the first slip stands to the right of the wicket keeper, but at an arm's distance. To the first slip's right, but, again, at an arm's distance, stands the second slip, then the third slip and so on.

Each slip fielder should keep his head still and concentrate fully on the outside edge of the bat (from where the catch will come), as if he could expect a catch from each delivery. If the bounce is low, the fielder can bend a little; if the bounce is high, he should maintain an upright stance. The exact fielding position would depend on the pace and bounce of the wicket.

Practice Methods for Catches in Slips

The device used to prepare the wicket, namely, the roller, can provide excellent practice in slip position catching. The fielder should stand behind the roller at a position where the ball, after impact, can reach him at an appropriate speed and at a reasonably comfortable height. Another player should throw the ball on top of the spherical surface of the roller so that the concerned fielder can take the catches on the other side. The cradle technique also provides good practice. At a suitable distance from the batsman, a slip cordon is formed. A player with a good throwing action (either underarm or overarm) flings the ball swiftly at the batsman from a short distance. The batsman then slices or slashes the ball to the slip fielders, thus providing good practice.

Gully

The gully also represents a specialised position on the off side. A fielder with swift reflexes and a keen sense of anticipation is positioned at gully. In this position, catches normally come off the hard, thick outside edge of the bat. After a slash stroke, the ball travels at a very high speed. Consequently, the fielder must know how far away he should stand. If the fielder observes that a particular batsman can cut the ball forcefully, then it is better that he stand a yard to two behind the normal fielding position so that he can get ample time for holding on to the catch.

With regard to the gully position, another point to be remembered is that catches can also come off mishit strokes such as cover drive, back foot drive or square cut. Therefore, the fielder must constantly concentrate on the bat angle.

Silly Point

In the olden days, there was no position as silly point. This position came into vogue in the seventies and since then it has proved instrumental in deciding the fate of many matches due to crucial catches being taken in this position. A fielder positioned at silly point can exert a lot of pressure on a defensive player to commit mistakes. To field at silly point, a player must have a lot of courage and also very quick reflexes. While fielding at silly point, the following points should be constantly kept in mind:

1. The fielder must not move, or anticipate the trajectory of the ball, *before* the batsman plays his stroke.
2. The catches will normally come off the bat and pad or off the gloves.
3. The fielder should watch the batsman carefully, concentrating on the bat angle while the latter is playing the stroke. Catches normally pop up when the batsman plays a faulty defensive stroke.
4. The fielder should be positioned such that he can catch the ball comfortably.
5. The fielder should be ever ready to take instant evasive action in case the batsman goes in for a powerful shot, lest the former gets injured.
6. The fielder should never take his eyes off the ball.
7. The fielder should wear adequate protective gear such as shin and abdominal guards and a helmet.

Silly Mid-off

A fielder normally occupies the silly mid-off position against defensive batsmen, especially when the latter comes forward time and time again to play a defensive stroke. Here, the catch usually comes off the bat and pad or sometimes even from the middle of the bat. Here too, the fielder should keep an eye on the batsman's foot movements and also concentrate on the bat angle.

Silly Mid-on

The silly mid-on position is frequently occupied when genuinely quick bowlers are operating. The purpose of stationing a fielder in this position is to put pressure on the batsman, when he is defending his wicket against a short rising delivery. The West Indian pace bowler Andy Roberts used to surprise a lot of batsmen with his sudden, short and rising deliveries, resulting in their spooning catches to the fielder at silly mid-on. Also, catches can come off the full face of the bat when a batsman tends to play forward. To repeat the obvious, the fielder should concentrate fully on the bat angle and the batsman's foot movements.

Leg Slip

Here, the catches generally come from the inside edge of the bat. Sometimes, catches may result as a result of the ball making contact with the full face of the bat, but being deflected towards the leg slip (positioned behind the batsman) as the batsman plays his stroke. Therefore, the fielder should keep a vigilant eye on the bat movement.

Short Leg

A fielder in the short leg position normally receives catches from bat-and-pad contact or glove contact. I have witnessed a lot of fielders taking catches at the short leg position but have not come across a better fielder than Eknath Solkar in this fairly dangerous position. He has snapped up amazing, almost impossible, catches which helped India win many crucial test matches. The short leg fielder has to be very courageous and also very nimble footed. He is bound to get hit and should hone his reflexes in order to take instant evasive action, whenever an extremely attacking stroke is played. The short leg fielder has, perforce, to crouch; the body weight should rest on the balls of the feet so that he can move freely to the left or right or even forward, if so needed.

The fielder's eyes should be focussed on the inside edge of the bat and as soon as the stroke has been played, the eyes should then concentrate on the trajectory of the ball so as to anticipate the catch perfectly. Obviously, sharp, split second reflexes and keen vision are essential. The fielder should adjust his position depending on the pace and bounce of the wicket.

Short Square Leg (Leg Gully)

The short square leg position is somewhat similar to the leg slip but slightly square. Here, too, catches normally come off the inside edge or full face of the bat, when the batsman plays a leg side stroke. Therefore, the fielder must concentrate carefully on the bat movements.

Other 'Short' Positions

Other short positions include short mid-on, short mid-wicket, short covers, short extra-covers and short mid-off. Such positions are, strictly speaking, not really close-in positions but fielders occupy them when the spinners are operating in order to snap up catches which may result due to mishit drives or miscued shots. Such positions are very effective in exerting pressure on the batsman to go in for the big hit and thus be snapped up in a deep position.

THE FLAT TRAJECTORY, HARD STRAIGHT CATCHES
These catches mostly come in the field area and sometimes in the slips area also. Such catches pop up at awkward heights, for instance, at chest height or head height. Normally, a fielder takes such difficult catches with both hands. In fact, he catches the ball with his strong hand, with the other hand serving as a support. However, when a flat trajectory, hard straight catch is taken, the fielder must make a little allowance in order to initially reduce or cut down the force of the ball so that the catch can be taken easily.

A fielder has to attempt the aforementioned catches by taking the catching hand slightly backwards, and by inverting the hand, with the fingers pointing upwards. The palm should be presented to the ball and the back of the hand should be towards the fielder's face. Such a catch is also known as a 'baseball catch'. The method just described is the only effective one for holding on to catches which pop up at awkward heights.

FIELDING GUIDELINES
As I have emphasised time and again, the fielder should keep his eyes constantly focussed on the ball and should always take the catch close to his body. He should not try to snatch the ball in mid-flight. A competent fielder always keeps his hands loose whenever he catches the ball. This is the reason why it appears as if he has 'swallowed' the ball with his hand as the ball sticks to his hand like a piece of iron sticks to a magnet.

I once had the opportunity of conversing with Mohammed Azharuddin during one of my TV programmes. I asked him as to what one should do to become a good fielder. His simple answer was that one should take at least 100 catches (during practice) every day in order to get used to the various trajectories of the ball. Whenever a fielder takes a catch, even during a practice session, he should do so as seriously as in a match.

One of the most common mistakes a fielder makes during a practice session is that he starts moving even before the batsman has played his stroke, especially in the outfield. Consequently, he reaches the ball much earlier. However, during matches, the vice versa holds true, i.e., the fielder is invariably late and tends to drop the catch, more often than not.

At this stage, let me provide a few basic guidelines for effective fielding in the somewhat deeper positions. The fielder should take a start along with the bowler and move towards the batsman so as to exert pressure on him and also try and reach the ball earlier by being ready to move quickly in any direction. Instead of walking upright, it is better to do so in a slightly crouched position, leaning forward a bit, in case it becomes necessary to bend down quickly to retrieve the ball.

Some fielders tend to walk rather casually (in an upright position) and some others tend to walk very fast, towards the batsman, with the result that both types are incorrectly positioned to take a catch. Therefore, the in between speed of movement becomes essential.

Let us now move on to discuss other positions in the field and their significance.

Cover Point

The cover point position is usually occupied by the most agile fielder in the team, who has the ability to save a lot of runs through his athletic prowess. A lot of practice has to be put in before one can acquire some degree of proficiency in the cover point position. A keen sense of anticipation is a must, because a fielder has to move quickly to the left or right, depending on the trajectory of the ball after the stroke. A fielder in the cover point position gets the chance of running out more batsmen than at any other position. A perceptive fielder can accurately judge the trajectory of the ball by carefully watching the face of the bat while the batsman is playing his shot. Such a fielder should also have the ability to bend rapidly, pick up the ball swiftly and hurl it accurately at the wicket, all in one smooth motion, while still running at a fairly high speed.

Mishit or miscued shots can also result in catches to the cover point fielder. Therefore, he should be alert and agile enough to accept such catches at any height. He may be required to run forward, backward or sideways and should be able to do so whenever the occasion demands.

Some of the outstanding cover fielders include Mansur Ali Khan Pataudi, Viv Richards, Derek Randall, Colin King, Paul Shehan, Clive Lloyd, David Gower, Jonty Rhodes, Salim Malik, Mohammed Azharuddin and Martin Crowe.

Extra-covers

The extra-covers position is next to the covers and requires the same approach as covers.

Mid-off

The mid-off position is one where most captains prefer to field, mainly because it helps them communicate easily with the bowlers. Moreover, this position provides them an overall view of the entire field. In the olden days, the mid-off position served as a 'rest' position for pace bowlers, but at present it is considered one of the key positions. The fielder in this position concentrates on the bat, whose full blade is used to hit the ball, when playing towards mid-off.

Mid-on

The mid-on position requires an energetic and athletic fielder, especially when pace bowlers are operating. This is because one only fielder is normally available to be stationed on the leg side in front of the wicket, who has to cover a wide area. My advice to a captain would be to never station a pace bowler or the key bowler at mid-on, because his fielding area is very large and he would soon become tired due to the excessive running and retrieving, and so would not be able to do justice to his bowling. In the mid-on position, the fielder should keenly concentrate on the bat movement, as the batsman would be playing more off the front foot.

Mid-wicket

The mid-wicket position is, again, a crucial one, like the covers. This position also requires an athletic and nimble-footed fielder, who can move swiftly both to his right and left. I have come across several batsmen who have misjudged the calibre of the fielder at mid-wicket and have fallen victims to run out. One particular instance is worth recalling, i.e., during the 1975 World Cup final, Viv Richards positioned at mid-wicket darted swiftly to his left and ran out Greg Chappell with a smart piece of fielding.

Square Leg

The square leg position is just behind the square leg umpire, which can, at times, become a catching position, depending on the fielder's precise position and the batsman's stroke. The ball comes towards this position more often when a pace bowler is operating. The moment the bowler deviates from his line on the leg side, the batsman gets an opportunity to hit with tremendous power. The fielder's main job would be to stop the ball. However, he should attempt catches whenever possible. The main disadvantage faced by the square leg fielder is that he cannot see the bat because the view is blocked by the batsman. Thus, it becomes very difficult for him to judge the trajectory and speed of the ball after the stroke has been played. The best course would be to keep one's eyes on the batsman's feet and try to follow the swing of the bat.

Short Third Man

The short third man position is a key fielding position, especially in one-day cricket. From this position many run outs have been achieved and several catches taken as a result of mishits. In this position, the fielder should have quick reflexes, because the ball tends to travel faster than expected in the case of mishits, resulting due to faulty execution of drives, square cuts or late cuts. The fielder in the third man position should concentrate on the bat movement as the ball would come off the outside edge when the batsman is playing his stroke.

THE OUTFIELD

In the olden days, the outfield positions or deep positions were considered to be 'relaxing positions' for tired fast bowlers. But this is not valid nowadays, because the standard and quality of fielding have gone up considerably. At present, athletic, energetic and diligent fielders, who can run fast and have a strong throwing arm, patrol the outfield areas, especially in one-day matches.

When stationed in a deep outfield position, a fielder cannot possibly prevent a single from being taken, but can try and stop the batsmen from taking more runs than one by moving quickly and throwing accurately at the wickets. Therefore, such a fielder should take a start along with the bowler so that he can reach the ball quickly, without any delay.

Sometimes, the boundary fielders tend to commit, some seemingly harmless mistakes, which could prove costly later. For instance, some fielders stand outside the boundary line, wave to the crowd and try to chat with some spectators. This can lead to a serious lapse of concentration. Also, it is safer to stand a few yards inside the boundary line so that the fielder can prevent extra runs from being taken.

As already stated, a competent fielder in the outfield must possess good speed and a strong throwing arm. One drawback I have noticed in Indian cricketers is that they do not get adequate throwing practice. As a result, when fielding in deep positions, they have to really struggle to hurl the ball properly. Only practice and more practice can eliminate this drawback.

HIGH CATCHES

All top-class fielders can take high catches easily. Such catches can appear at any part of the field, depending on the stroke played by the batsman. There are two methods of taking high catches: (1) The traditional English style and (2) the baseball method. Both are equally effective.

The first method is an ideal one, and in this method, the fielder uses both hands to make a 'big basket' to catch the ball safely and comfortably (Fig. 4.7).

Fig. 4.7 The 'big basket' method

In the second method, the palm of the strong hand (facing outwards) is used to take the catch, with the other hand providing the necessary support. High catches are normally taken at chest height.

High catches are sometimes very difficult to take although the ball may seem to linger in the air for a long time. This is because the fielder has to constantly look up and simultaneously run towards the anticipated spot where the ball would fall. Sometimes, one has to run sideways or backwards for taking a high catch, adding to the degree of difficulty. At times, sunlight (or artificial bright lights) could obstruct the vision. The following guidelines would prove useful while attempting a high catch:

1. The head should be kept steady, even while running, with the eyes keeping track of the ball's trajectory to the extent possible.
2. A fielder should not blindly rush in to take a high catch. He should first locate the ball in the air, then follow its flight and move as quickly as possible into a position to snap up the catch.
3. The ball should be taken at chest height and close to the chest.
4. For the 'big basket' catch, the fingers should be well spread out, and pointing towards the sky. To make a 'big basket', the small finger of the right hand should remain on top of the small finger of the other hand. The catch should be taken in the strong hand. As soon as the fielder catches the ball, he should bring his hand to his chest, with palms facing the chest.
5. The hand should be kept sufficiently loose, so that the ball can 'stick in' easily.

DROPPED CATCHES

A fielder usually drops a catch as a result of one or a combination of the following factors:

1. He keeps his hands extremely stiff while attempting the catch.
2. He shifts the ball away from the body on to the head or the face.
3. His fingers are not adequately spread out to latch on to the catch.
4. He does not pick up the trajectory or flight of the ball accurately and just blindly rushes in to take the catch and, that too, very early.
5. He runs too fast; consequently, he is unable to keep his head steady and it starts wobbling, making him lose sight of the ball.

To round off this chapter, let me cite a revealing anecdote to stress the crucial role of fielding in deciding the fate of a match. Once, while playing in a Benson and Hedges match against Australia in 1986, we (India) managed to bowl out our opponents rather cheaply and thought that scoring the required runs to win would be a 'cakewalk'. But to our surprise, the Australian fielders put up tremendous resistance. They darted and dived all over the place to save a run, wherever possible, and applied intense pressure on us. Ultimately, the Aussies won by a narrow margin. This incident tellingly reveals the wonders that determined and diligent fielding can achieve.

Five
Bowling Allies

Bowling constitutes a vital aspect of the game of cricket. Over the years, many players have shot to fame on the basis of their bowling abilities. The prominent names that spring to mind immediately are: Keith Miller, Harold Larwood, Mohd. Nissar, Ray Lindwall, Jim Laker, Vinod Mankad, Wesley Hall, Lance Gibbs, Dennis Lillee, E.A.S. Prasanna, B.S. Chandrashekhar, B.S. Bedi, S. Venkataraghavan, Kapil Dev, Sir Richard Hadlee, Ian Botham, Bob Willis, Andy Roberts, Malcolm Marshall, Michael Holding, Joel Garner, Imran Khan, Abdul Qadir, Wasim Akram and Waqar Younis. Of course, there are several other bowlers, whose talent and potential are noteworthy, but it is not possible to mention every one of them here.

I myself started my career as a pace bowler at a very young age, and managed to achieve a fair amount of success. As a matter of fact, I played my first test match (against Australia in 1969) as a pace bowler. I can still vividly recall the joy and satisfaction I had derived when I captured my first test wicket (i.e., of Keith Stackpole). However, I did not achieve success overnight; I had to really slog and put in long hours of hard work and toil before I could make my mark. I remember the gruelling net practice sessions; the sweat; the grime; the intense efforts; and above all, the dedicated perseverance, which ultimately helped me accomplish all that I could.

Sometimes, in the world of cricket, bowlers have been treated as 'villains' and batsmen as 'heroes' because only one batsman, at a time, seems to be fighting 11 opposing players (and sometimes hostile ones at that)! However, I think this view is incorrect and unjustified. Bowlers are merely playing the game to the best of their abilities, and it is not their fault that the rules of the game are such that only one batsman at a time can play the ball. In fact, in several matches, bowlers have proved instrumental in achieving victory.

The West Indies dominated world cricket, especially in the bowling department, from 1976 to 1985. Their team invariably consisted of a minimum of four accomplished pace bowlers. During an exhibition match in New York during the 1991-92 tour, I once had a chance to talk to West Indian paceman Colin Croft. He told me that during the aforesaid years, although the West Indies rarely managed to pile up huge totals, a score of 250-300 was good enough for achieving victory because of their penetrating and effective bowling attack.

Most fast bowlers do not exactly earn a great deal of affection because of their aggressive and belligerent attitude towards the game, towards the opposing batsmen, and sometimes towards the umpires. Some of them tend to hurl the choicest invectives and rather loudly at that. In this sort of behaviour on the field, the Australians are the leaders. On the contrary, the quietest and most well-behaved players are the West Indians. I have played a lot of cricket against the West Indies teams, but rarely ever did they get into any argument or altercation.

Coming back to the main topic, bowling can be divided into two broad categories: (1) pace bowling and (2) spin bowling.

PACE BOWLING

Pace bowling can be further subdivided into (1) genuine pace, (2) medium fast and (3) medium pace. Whether a bowler opts for pace or spin, his main aim should be to make the batsman play forward. My father, the great all-rounder, Shri Lala Amarnath, constantly reminded me that the bowler who pitches the ball up to the batsman, and makes him play forward, would achieve maximum success. This is because batsmen tend to make more mistakes while playing off the front foot rather than the back foot. If a batsman tends to play more off the back foot than the front foot, this means that he is comfortable with the bowling. Such bowling lacks lustre and penetration. Ideally, a bowler in his follow through should be looking at the batsman over his right shoulder. This indicates that the bowler has bowled a good delivery with good line and control.

Let me now cite a few real-life examples to illustrate my arguments.

Imran Khan was very quick in the 1977-78 series between India and Pakistan, but he was not very successful. The main reason was that he was pitching the ball too short most of the time. After a couple of years, he changed his tactics and started pitching the ball up to the batsmen. As a result, he was able to attain more movement to bowl his lethal inswingers effectively. Michael Holding also became more accurate and successful after he started pitching the ball up to the batsman. Waqar Younis (Pakistan) provides a perfect example of how to pitch the ball up to the batsman and thus increase one's strike rate considerably. In other words, a successful bowler is one who makes the batsman play forward.

During the good old days, coaches did not pay much attention to using bowling as a strategic weapon; instead, they would instruct the bowlers to merely concentrate on good line and length. But over the years the trend has changed. It has come to be realised that bowlers can win matches and coaches must provide the required training and practice.

Planning plays an important role in bowling. Depending on the wicket, the weather conditions and the situation of the match, a bowler must plan his overall strategy, with due provision for improvisation, whenever required. The thrill and the enjoyment provided by getting a batsman out through proper planning are something that can only be felt, not described.

Practice also plays an important role in ensuring a bowler's success. Even during a net session, the bowler should concentrate totally on his bowling as if he were playing in a match. During net sessions, pace bowlers tend to overstep and this can generate a lot of pace and movement (due to the shorter distance). However, once they start playing a match, they are pulled up for 'no balls'. Thus, one must be cautious enough to avoid committing this error.

Normally, pace bowlers are hefty and sturdy in physique. However, if one does not have the build of a tank, there is no need to get disheartened! Spin bowling could help in bagging as many wickets as pace bowling, if not more!

In my opinion, a good pace bowler is one who can come back and bowl equally effectively in the third or fourth spell. Any fast bowler can bowl well when the ball is new and he is fresh. However, it calls for a great deal of grit, hard work and fitness for a bowler to perform equally well during his last spell (as during the first spell).

Another point to be remembered is that if an aspiring bowler wants to learn a new technique or tactic, he should first try it out at the nets and achieve some degree of perfection before utilising it in a match. If a bowler attempts something new straightaway in a match, he could be hit all over the place and may become demoralised. In this context, one incident comes to my mind. Sunil Valson (a member of the 1983 World Cup team) was playing a domestic match in Bombay. The team manager showed him certain grips just before the start of play, and the poor chap tried them out straightaway! He just could not bowl straight and maintain his line and length. He finally decided to switch over to his original grip, after which he picked up crucial wickets and his side won the match.

One should remain a student of the game always and should try to learn a lot by watching a competent bowler in action.

THE BASICS OF BOWLING

The discussion here pertains to a right-hand bowler. Broadly, a left-hand bowler should do the opposite mentioned here (of course, exceptions would depend on individual situations).

A majority of right-hand bowlers tend to bowl over the wicket to attain better control over, and movement of, the ball. The basic aim of a bowler should be to make the batsman play each and every delivery. No batsman in the world would be happy to play all the six balls in an over, that too, over after over. In this respect, Sir Richard Hadlee has been the most accurate and successful bowler due to his immense concentration and control.

Bowling is comparatively easier than batting because the bowler can get another chance, whereas if a batsman commits a fatal error, he has to go back to the pavilion! (All my sympathies are with the batsman!) Moreover, a bowler can bag a wicket with a bad delivery but a batsman invariably falls victim to bad shot!

Why I claim that bowling is easier than batting is because a bowler doesn't really need a batsman to practise with. For instance, Narendra Hirwani (a leg spinner who had a dream-come-true debut against the West Indies, amassing 16 wickets in one match) once told me that he used to practise with a single wicket (and of course a wicket-keeper). He used to place a handkerchief or some other marker at the good length spot and try to constantly hit that spot to gain control and achieve accuracy.

Bowling consists of the following four main factors: (1) grip; (2) run-up; (3) action; and (4) follow through.

The aforementioned four factors apply to both pace bowling and spin bowling. Naturally, there are a lot of variations on each of the basics in order to produce different kinds of deliveries. Every successful bowler possesses 'a bag of tricks' (in the form of subtle variations) in order to surprise a batsman and coerce him to commit an error.

Grip

Grip (Fig. 5.1) plays a significant part in ensuring success for a bowler. It is more useful to have a finger grip rather than a palm grip, because the former helps in providing a good deal of variation.

Fig. 5.1 The basic grip

Checklist

1. Normally, the thumb and the first finger make the shape of a 'V' and there is a noticeable gap between them.
2. The first two fingers lie apart along the seam.
3. The thumb comes directly beneath the first two fingers (of course, the position changes depending on the type of delivery).
4. The third finger rests lightly as a support to the ball (so that it does not fall down).
5. While holding the ball, the grip should feel comfortable, because if it is too tight or too loose, one cannot really bowl effectively.

Run-up

Whether one is a pace bowler or a spinner, a smooth run-up is necessary. The main objectives of the run-up are to help the bowler move into his delivery stride and to provide the necessary momentum, both of which lead to his delivering the ball effectively and accurately. Most of the great bowlers possess a rhythmic momentum, which helps them bowl beautifully. In fact, Michael Holding (West Indies) was known as the 'Rolls Royce' of fast bowlers because of his flawless, easy run-up. Such a run-up helped him to bowl really fast with a minimum of effort. I remember one incident when playing against Holding in the West Indies in 1976. When he came on to bowl, practically the entire Indian team was standing on the pavilion balcony to watch his run-up.

I strongly believe that half of a bowler's capability depends on his run-up. A too short or too long run-up does not help a bowler in getting the proper rhythm. All bowlers must spend a good deal of time in perfecting their run-up, which, inevitably, varies from one bowler to another.

Checklist
1. Before commencing the actual act of bowling, a bowler should measure his run-up distance from the bowling crease and keep a marker at the point from which he intends to begin his run-up.
2. While starting the run-up, the bowler's body weight should be in front; the bowler should initially take small strides and gradually lengthen them, simultaneously increasing his speed gradually.
3. The bowler should follow the same run-up pattern again and again to achieve the required momentum and rhythm.
4. The bowler should preferably carry the ball in his bowling arm.
5. All the great fast bowlers take long strides in order to obtain the required momentum. While running, their heels almost touch the bottom of their hip, providing a better rhythm.
6. While running, the bowler should look at the batsman, bearing in mind the exact spot where he intends to pitch the ball. This decision should, in fact, be made prior to commencing the run-up. A common error that bowlers commit is that they change their mind just before delivering the ball, resulting in a lot of confusion.
7. The head should always remain steady so that the bowler can carefully follow the trajectory of the ball.

Action

Once the bowler (i.e., pace bowler) has developed the required momentum and before he reaches the bowling crease, he should leap (or bound) in the air and turn his front (left) shoulder to the right side so as to get into a sideways position. On landing on the ground after the leap (or bound), the right toe should be parallel to the bowling crease. For achieving the maximum effect, the following points should be borne in mind:

1. The leap or bound is a link between run-up and delivery. At the time of delivery, it is important to lean back to the maximum extent possible and make an arch of the back. This helps the fast bowler to achieve the maximum momentum through the delivery stride.

2. As the bowler lands on the ground after the leap or bound, he should get into the 'coil position'. In this position, the body leans back, the front foot is raised high and the front arm is positioned as high as possible but without blocking the bowler's view. At this point, the bowler should be looking over his left shoulder at the precise spot where he intends to pitch the ball. The bowling hand is held high (up to the chest), just below the chin. (See Fig. 5.2.)

Fig. 5.2   Bowling action

3. It is important for the bowler to maintain a sideways position. Too long or too short a delivery stride could lead to the bowler losing his balance and momentum.

4. As the bowler comes through the final delivery stride, the body weight is transferred from the right leg to the left leg, which is slightly flexed in order to take the impact created by the bowling action. The wrist is cocked back to give maximum speed to the ball.

5. The front foot is kept in the line of the back foot. The bowling arm should be held high and straight in order to obtain the desired bounce.

6. When the bowler delivers the ball his right arm finishes near the left ribs and left arm goes high in the air, leading to complete body action.

Follow Through

Most of the successful pace bowlers have a smooth follow through. The West Indian pace bowler Andy Roberts had a very good and rhythmic run-up to the wicket, but after delivering the ball, he used to finish his follow through close to silly mid-off and sometimes he had to literally apply brakes to stop himself. This showed how much effort he was putting into his bowling.

After delivering the ball, the bowler could pivot on his front foot and try to twist his hips in such a way as to move out of the line of the wickets. The bowler should remember that he has to avoid stepping one foot on either side of the middle stump and 4 feet from the batting crease.

The bowler should look over his right shoulder during the follow through to know exactly where the ball has pitched.

FOCUS ON PACE BOWLING

Let us move on to some other aspects of pace bowling. Pace bowlers generally possess a robust and strong physique, a good height, powerful shoulders, sturdy legs and a firm back. Although many Indian players have possessed these characteristics, and still do, very few have achieved success in the field of fast bowling. This is mainly because the coaches hardly allow or encourage anyone to bowl fast. If someone bowls fast with a wayward line he would be asked to concentrate only on his line and length rather than on pace along with line and length. Consequently, such a bowler may become dispirited and lose his talent as well as his morale. In this connection, I recall the example of Pandurang Salgonkar from Maharashtra. He was a strong and sturdily built chap and bowled pretty fast, with a slightly roundish action. He did very well in unofficial test matches in Sri Lanka in 1974 but was not picked for the following tour of England because the selectors thought he would not prove successful. However, later on, he was sent to England for training (in order to improve his bowling action), which resulted in his losing pace and we lost a quick bowler. I am sure that if Salgonkar had been guided properly he would have proved to be an asset to Indian cricket.

It has always been a treat to watch a fast bowler in full cry. I can assure my readers that no batsman would be happy to play quick bowlers the whole day, and, in the process, be subjected to a constant volley of tremendously swift deliveries. You can well imagine how a batsman must feel when the ball zooms towards him at about 140 km per hour! It isn't a particularly comforting feeling! I personally think that the excitement, tension and drama that a fast bowler can create cannot be matched by any other department of the game. The thrill and the pleasure one derives by just watching the pacemen such as Holding, Imran, Waqar Younis and Wasim Akram in full flow are qualitatively different from those obtained by watching class batsmen executing their strokes.

Many young and hopeful cricketers would like to become fast bowlers, but very few have the physique and temperament. Therefore, it is important to locate and develop youngsters who have the requisite physique and the right temperament and the ability to bowl fast. Such prospective talent should be properly nurtured and guided so as to emerge as prime strike bowlers. To state the obvious, a great deal of practice and perseverance are needed as also the determination and ambition to succeed.

If you, as an individual, think that you possess the capability to bowl fast, then initially, just concentrate on bowling as fast as you can; other types of deliveries such as swingers and cutters can be learnt later on. Youngsters today want to learn everything at once, resulting in confusion and bewilderment. Consequently, they could lose whatever ability they initially possessed. Therefore, a systematic step-by-step approach is needed to develop the qualities of a genuine pace bowler, which include aggression, self-confidence and an ability to keep cool despite the exertion and the pressures of the game. Also, proper physical training and complete physical fitness are essential, which help any player in extending his career. The outstanding examples are Imran, Hadlee, Marshall, Lillee, Botham and our own Kapil Dev.

Let us now take up different aspects of pace bowling individually.

Swing Bowling (Medium Pace)

The main point to be noted is that genuine fast bowlers do not swing the ball as much as the medium pacemen do. All fiercely fast bowlers tend to concentrate on speed, and swing has always been secondary to them. On the other hand, medium pacers concentrate on swinging the ball and become proficient in more than one type of swing in order to achieve variation in their attack. In my opinion, it is comparatively easier to play genuine pacemen rather than swing bowlers. Kapil Dev, Botham, Hadlee and Imran concentrated on their swing bowling and thus emerged successful. In fact, Imran proved more penetrating and effective once he began mixing swing with genuine pace.

Swing bowlers usually go in for three types of deliveries, depending on their skills and abilities.

1. Those deliveries that move in the air.
2. Those deliveries that land on the seam of the ball and move to the right or left.
3. Those deliveries (called 'cutters') which result when the bowler drags his fingers across the ball while bowling and the ball, after hitting the ground, moves to the off side or leg side.

Why does the ball swing or swerve in the air? The reason is as follows: The stitches on the outer surface of the ball create a ridge around its circumference. The movement imparted by the bowler's fingers and also the different atmospheric conditions exert different kinds of forces on the ridge, causing the ball to move in one direction or the other. It is important to give some air to the ball because the longer it is in the air, the more it will swing. (See Fig. 5.3.) That's why a medium pacer can move the ball more than a fast bowler. A heavy, overcast atmosphere along with humidity and breezes helps in moving the ball appreciably.

g spinner Anil Kumble displays his
owling wiles

Sir Richard Hadlee in full flow

K. Srikkanth plays a powerful shot

'King' Richards executes a lofted drive

The agile Jonty Rhodes leaps to catch the ball

Alan Lamb run out by alert Indian fielders

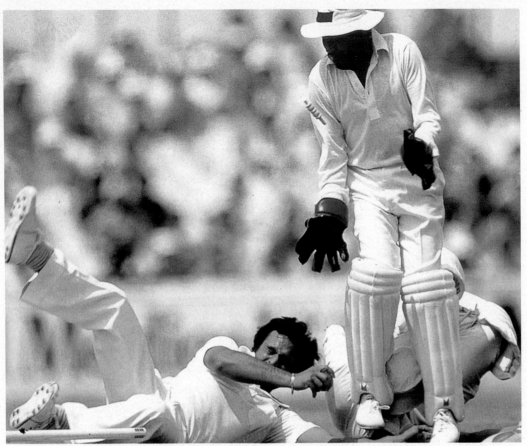

Wicket-keeper Syed Kirmani claims a victim

Jeff Dujon exhibits acrobatic wicket-keeping

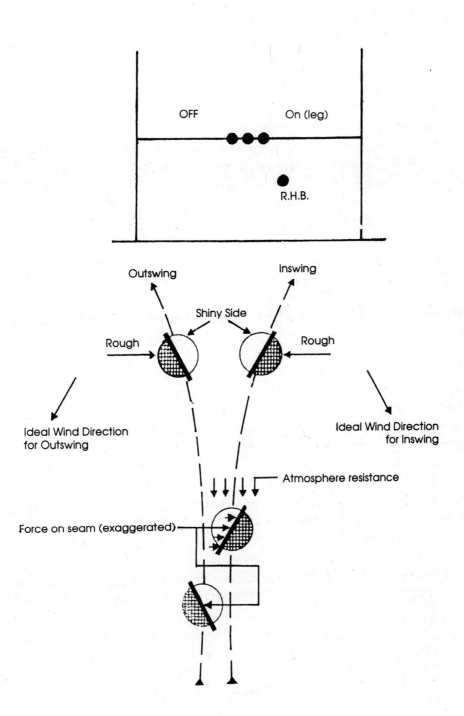

Fig 5.3 Swing bowling diagrammatically explained

Bowlers must keep on experimenting with their grip to obtain sufficient variation, which they can effectively employ to increase or curtail the swing in order to fox the batsmen. All great bowlers possess a stock of 'quick' or 'slow' deliveries. The late Sir Larry Constantine of the West Indies used to baffle batsmen by suddenly bowling a googly (explained later in this chapter) as a change of pace during hostile fast bowling.

All bowlers should make full use of the bowling crease, which can lead to a lot of variation and movement in their bowling. A bowler should not deliver each and every ball from the same spot, when a fairly long bowling crease is available. He should take optimum advantage of its length to puzzle and trouble the batsmen. (This applies to both pace and spin bowlers.) Bowling is not restricted to simply picking up the ball and bowling it; it also includes taking care of the ball, by 'shining' it on one's trousers, to maintain its newness to the extent possible.

There are two possible types of swing, namely, (1) outswing and (2) inswing. In outswing bowling, the ball swings towards the off side slips and in inswing bowling, it is vice versa.

Outswing Bowling

Outswing bowlers have been highly successful in all varieties of cricket because most batsmen find outswing bowling difficult to deal with. Even the all-time greats such as Viv Richards, Sunil Gavaskar and Javed Miandad encountered problems while facing an outgoing delivery, mainly during the beginning of the innings. During outswing bowling, the cordon of slip fielders is enhanced to accept any possible catch.

While bowling to a right-handed batsman, the bowler should try to bowl from a spot close to the stumps in order to get maximum swing and body action into the delivery. He should always try and make the batsman play forward, again, making optimum use of the bowling crease to bring about variation (and surprises) in the bowling pattern.

Checklist
1. The bowler should bowl from close to the stumps, looking over his left shoulder, with the eyes focussed on the target and the head kept perfectly still.
2. At the time of delivery, the seam should be facing the slips (off side) or third man and the palm should also face the same direction.
3. While gripping the ball, the first two fingers should be on both sides (i.e., one on each side) of the seam, with the inside of the thumb touching the seam underneath. The knuckles should be facing the bowler (Fig. 5.4).

4. The aforementioned two fingers should be positioned behind the ball at the instant of release; the ball should be released with a firm wrist action in a straight direction.

Fig. 5.4 The girp for outswing

5. The bowler should try to bowl side-on, i.e., with the right foot parallel to the bowling crease and the left foot facing the fine leg position. While delivering the ball, the bowler should pivot on his front foot, twist his hips and swing his right arm vigorously across his body. (Some bowlers tend to move their left foot across the right foot.)

6. After delivery, ideally, the right arm finishes somewhere near the left ribs and the left arm is raised high in the air so as to provide maximum body movement.

7. Immediately after delivering the ball, the bowler should turn to his left and move out of the wickets so that he doesn't leave any foot marks there.

8. The bowler should lean back (i.e., make an arch with his body) before delivery and later attain a coil position to achieve maximum impact. Kapil Dev, Richard Hadlee and Dennis Lillee are ideal models in this context.

Kapil Dev once told me that different bowlers have different grips for the outswinger. However, the basic objective should be to release the ball in a straight direction and make sure that the seam lands on the ground.

Inswing Bowling

Two of the finest inswing bowlers I have seen in world cricket hail from Pakistan, namely, Imran Khan and Waqar Younis. The amount of swing that these bowlers have been able to generate is truly amazing. The reason for this can be attributed to their body action as also to their tremendous efforts. They have a fast rhythmic run-up. They leap up and attain a good height and remain side-on while bowling, but at the instant of delivery, they drop or open their left shoulder a bit in order to induct maximum body action (for achieving a large amount of swing).

For inswing bowling, the grip (Fig. 5.5) varies from that for outswing bowling; although the seam stays vertical, but instead of facing third man, it faces the leg slip or fine leg.

Fig. 5.5 *The grip for inswing*

Checklist

1. The bowler's first two fingers stay on either side of the seam and the thumb lies flat against the seam.

2. To obtain a proper inswing grip, the bowler should ensure that, while gripping the ball, the knuckles of the first two fingers are facing upwards.

3. During inswing bowling, the bowler looks at the batsman from the inside of the left shoulder, keeping the left arm high.

4. The bowler should maintain a side-on position, with the back foot parallel to the bowling crease, but if this foot is not parallel, there is nothing wrong; what is more important is to achieve more swing and body action.
5. The bowler should keep his head still, with the eyes on the target.
6. As mentioned earlier, while gripping the ball, the seam should be facing the leg slip or fine leg, with the wrist towards the same direction. The bowling arm should come straight across and maintain a high action.
7. Ideally, after the delivery, the right arm should finish somewhere near the left' ribs, with the left arm raised high. In some cases, the right arm may end up between the bowler's legs and the left arm may not be raised very high. Such situations do not really matter as long as one is able to achieve the requisite swing.
8. For the outswinger, at the time of delivery, the left elbow is tucked under the left ribs, whereas for the inswinger, the left arm stays away from the body, enabling the body to rotate easily.
9. After the ball has been delivered, the bowler should keep his eyes on the ball during his follow through, looking over his right shoulder to know exactly where it pitches so that he can anticipate the batsman's response.

Seam Bowling

Seam bowling can prove to be highly effective and successful on damp, grassy and green wickets, which help the ball move in either direction after pitching. The basic aim of a seam bowler is to try and pitch the ball on the vertical seam so that he could move it either way, as desired. For achieving such perfection, one has to bowl very accurately.

The grip for seam bowling is not very much different from the basic grip. The main difference is that, in seam bowling, the bowler drags his fingers back on the seam (instead of letting go of the ball straight from his hand) for obtaining swing and swerve. In England, present-day cricketers seam the ball more because of the ideal conditions. The prominent names associated with seam bowling are Sarfaraz Nawaz, Mike Hendricks, Chris Old and, of late, Chris Cairns (New Zealand).

Cutters

Every successful pace bowler or medium pacer stocks a variety of 'weapons' in his armoury. All the great bowlers employ a combination of swing and cutters. For instance, Kapil Dev and Sir Richard Hadlee could beautifully mix the offcutter with the outwinger. Also, Imran Khan could nip in with outswingers and leg cutters along with his 'banana inswinger' (i.e., a big inswinger).

When bowling a cutter, the bowler's fingers are dragged along the side of the ball, so as to generate clockwise or anticlockwise spin, as required. Normally, the first two fingers are used for this purpose. On damp wickets, cutters can prove devastating.

Sometimes, even on dry wickets, cutters can be used to rattle the batsmen.

There are two types of cutters, namely, off cutters and leg cutters. I have noticed that outswing bowlers tend to bowl good off cutters and inswing bowlers are skilful at bowling lovely leg cutters.

Off Cutters

The grip for the off cutter (Fig. 5.6) is somewhat similar to that for the outswinger. The difference is that, in this case, the first finger comes close to the seam and the second finger is a bit away (wider), with the thumb resting on the side of the ball instead of under the seam. The mode of action is more or less similar to the outswinger, with the basic difference that the first two fingers cut across the ball, the first finger pulling the seam down, clockwise.

As I have stressed several times, it is essential for a bowler to possess a variety of attack because if he concentrates on just one type of delivery, a good batsman can easily tackle it after judging its line and length. However, if the bowler can ingeniously vary his attack, blending off cutters and outswingers, even if he pitches wide off the stumps, he can compel the batsman to play his strokes and thus commit an error, which could result in a catch to the slips or in his being clean bowled. Ideally, the bowler should pitch the ball up to the batsman and pitch it on, or slightly outside, the off stump, forcing the batsman to play a shot.

There is one other technique for bowling the off cutter. The grip is the same as mentioned earlier, but, at the

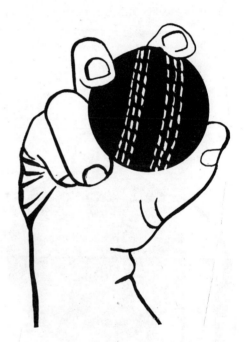

Fig. 5.6 The off cutter grip

instant of delivery, the bowler presses the ball down, clockwise, with his first finger, so that, after pitching, the ball comes into the right-handed batsman.

Leg Cutters

The grip for bowling leg cutters (Fig. 5.7) is somewhat similar to that for inswingers. The only change is that the bowler slides the first finger down, with the second finger resting on the seam. After pitching, the ball moves away from the batsman (usually towards the off side slips). As I have mentioned earlier, a competent inswing bowler can bowl incisive leg cutters because he does not have to change his grip very much.

In the olden days, Alec Bedser of England attained great proficiency in delivering the leg cutter. After that very few bowlers have put the leg cutter to maximum use among whom rank Malcolm Marshall, Courtney Walsh and Curty Ambrose, all from the West Indies.

My father, Lala Amarnath, used to employ the leg cutter as a surprise delivery with telling effect. The top batsmen of his time used to get caught or bowled while playing across the line of the ball. He proved very successful with his inswingers and leg cutters during the 1946 Indian tour of England.

Checklist

1. A bowler requires full body action in order to perfect the leg cutter. The fingers, hips and the front foot (for pivoting) play an important role. At the time of delivery, the second finger pulls the seam in an anticlockwise direction and the thumb assists in this process by twisting the ball as it is released.

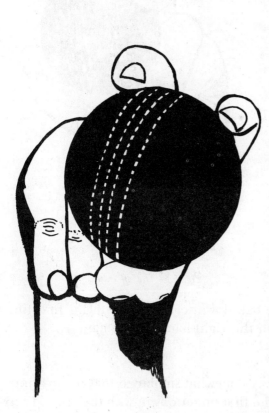

2. At the time of delivery, the seam points towards fine leg, when the bowler rolls his finger on top of it to obtain the necessary direction. The left toe also points in the fine leg direction. The pivoting of the front foot is essential to rotate the hips, enabling the body to twist and turn. When bowling the leg cutter, the bowler gets the feeling that he is pushing the ball down the leg side. It is important to pitch the ball up, on the stumps, so that it can move the other way after pitching.

Fig. 5.7 The leg cutter grip

By now, I hope my young (and not so young) readers would have acquired a fairly good knowledge about pace bowling. However, merely theoretical knowledge is not enough. All aspiring cricketers should practise and practise hard at that. They should identify their weak points and try and eliminate them. One should remember that all the great bowlers did not achieve success overnight; they had to toil and work hard for years, with dedication and perseverance.

SPIN BOWLING

Spin bowling is nothing short of an art. One of the most rewarding experiences for a spin bowler would be to fool a batsman with a seemingly harmless flighted delivery, inviting the latter to come down the wicket and take a swipe at it, and suddenly finding himself stranded as the ball spins away from him and he is convincingly stumped. Cricket is not merely an awesome and ferocious display of pace bowling; it also involves the subtle guile of spin. In fact, Indian spinners by themselves have enabled their team to win many matches with their dextrous and clever bowling.

Spin bowling can be broadly divided into three categories, namely, leg spin, left arm spin and off spin. But before discussing the details, let me first dwell upon the famous spinners of the cricket world. India has produced some of the greatest spinners, who dominated the international cricket scene for a number of years.

The outstanding example of the leg spinner B.S. Chandrashekhar achieving victory virtually single handed at the Oval Test (against England in 1971) comes to my mind whenever spin bowling is discussed. The other luminaries in the Indian spin department include the inimitable Bishen Singh Bedi, E.A.S. Prasanna and S. Venkataraghavan. I recollect one series against Australia in 1968-69 in which Bedi and Prasanna simply ran through the formidable batting line-up. Also, the Bedi-Prasanna-Chandra trio ensured India's comeback in a series against the West Indies in 1974-75, after being 2-0 down.

When I was playing in my first test (in 1969), the spinners were really dominating the scene, at least in India. The captain instructed me not to polish the ball (as is customary for fast bowlers or medium pacers to do) because I would be bowling only a few overs merely to complete the formalities.

When spinners are operating, the level of activity in the field goes up considerably. The fun and excitement increase. More overs are bowled and more action is seen — either runs are scored or wickets fall. I have enjoyed playing with and against Bedi, Prasanna and Chandrashekhar. It was always an edifying experience to watch how they trapped their victims through guile, subtlety and patience.

Both India and Pakistan have produced accomplished spinners because of the nature of wickets and the weather conditions in the subcontinent. Leg spinners, though a bit of a rarity, have gained a great deal of acclaim; for instance, B.S. Chandrashekhar, Abdul Qadir (Pakistan), Narendra Hirwani, and, of late, Anil Kumble, Mushtaq Ahmed (Pakistan) and Shane Warne (Australia). Among the older lot, Richie Benaud won a lot of matches for Australia.

Chandrashekhar and Qadir could emerge successful because of their deceptive ability to baffle the batsmen with their spin. At times, the batsmen just could not figure out which way the ball was going to turn after pitching.

A leg spinner can bowl three types of deliveries with almost the same grip and action, which is quite a challenge to the batsman! These three deliveries are (1) the leg spin, (2) the googly and (3) the flipper or the straight ball.

Leg Spin

Leg spinners normally constitute a bunch of attacking bowlers, although they could prove a bit expensive. However, they are basically wicket takers compared to other types of spinners. Leg spinners prefer good wickets to prove their mettle and end up with a rich haul of wickets in many matches.

A leg spin delivery is one which turns from the leg stump (or just outside) towards the off stump when bowled to a right-hand batsman (i.e., anticlockwise). In other words, it is a delivery which *leaves* the batsman. If the batsman wants to step forward and execute a stroke on the on side, he would be playing *against* the spin. Therefore, utmost caution is required while tackling a leg spinner. No wonder, any good captain would definitely love to include a leg spinner in the team. Let me cite a few examples. The track record of leg spinner Chandrashekhar is truly remarkable. Imran Khan also frequently relied on Abdul Qadir to deliver the goods. Sunil Gavaskar selected a young leg spinner named Sivaramakrishnan, who helped in winning the World Series in Australia in 1985. Similarly, Mushtaq Ahmed played a crucial role in bagging the World Cup for Pakistan in 1992.

Grip

For leg spin, the ball is gripped between the first three fingers (Fig. 5.8). The first two fingers are spaced apart and hold the ball across the seam. The third finger is bent in such a way that it lies along the seam. The thumb rests lightly on the ball and does not play any part in spinning the ball. The third finger is the crucial finger as it has to ultimately spin the ball. The ideal way of getting a firm spin grip is to open one's palm, space out the first two fingers and then put in the ball into the so-formed cup. As you grip the ball, bend the third finger suitably to lie along the seam.

Fig. 5.8 Leg spin grip

Action

Before a bowler actually bowls, he should first measure out his run-up distance accurately. This distance should not be too short or too long; it should be sufficient enough to provide a rhythmic run-up and a smooth action delivery. After determining the precise distance, a marker should be kept at the starting point.

Checklist
1. The bowler's run-up should be smooth and easy. It's better to adopt a diagonal run-up so that the bowler can assume the side-on position easily and attain full body movement at the time of delivery.

2. The right foot should be parallel to the bowling crease. The final stride should be fairly long. The left toe should point towards fine leg to take on a side-on position.

3. The bowler should be looking over his left shoulder to know exactly where the ball has pitched.

4. The wrist should be bent inwards prior to the delivery and at the time of delivery, the third finger is dragged along the seam in an anticlockwise direction. The right arm stays high and straight.

5. At the time of delivery, the bowler's left leg should go slightly across with respect to the back leg. Then, the bowler should pivot on to his left foot, twist his hips (fully) leftwards and transfer his body weight from the right leg to the left leg. He should move to the left of the wicket (to avoid running on to it).

6. The bowler should always keep his eyes on the ball and should remain ready to field to his own bowling, if required. As leg spin bowling is fairly aggressive, one must make allowance for a follow through.

7. The ball usually pitches on or outside the leg stump and moves towards the off side slips.

Googly

The googly is a fairly tricky and secretive delivery. It is a very useful weapon if employed adroitly by a leg spinner. A googly is essentially an off break bowled in the guise of a leg break by a right-hand bowler to a right-hand batsman. It's thrilling

for a bowler to get a batsman out by a googly as a result of subtle deception. I have seen a lot of batsmen (when facing a leg spinner) play for the leg spin, but to their surprise (and horror), they have found the ball to spin the other way, resulting in their being bowled or offering a catch. The googly is not easy to bowl as its spin is hard to control. It requires a great deal of practice, day after day, to master this delivery. The googly is basically a wrist action delivery, although the first two fingers do have a role to play as also the back of the hand (see Fig. 5.9).

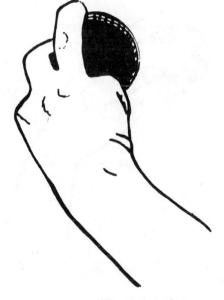

Fig. 5.9 The googly grip

Checklist
1. When the bowler begins his run-up, ideally, he should be looking at the batsman. At the same time, he should have a fairly accurate idea of where exactly to pitch the ball for the googly to be effective. During the process of bowling, the bowler should drop his left shoulder, and, at the time of delivery, he should show only the back of his hand to the batsman (in order to conceal the googly). The bowler uses a bent wrist and flips the ball with the third finger at the instant of delivery. The ball comes out of the back of the hand, over the third and fourth fingers.
2. The googly is bowled with a comparatively open chested action. The bowling arm goes up, straight and high, more or less touching the right ear. A good deal of strain is imposed on the right shoulder.
3. The bowler's follow through lies in the line of the batsman because he has to twist his arm to such an extent that it becomes very difficult for him to turn to the left.
4. The googly should be pitched slightly away from the off stump so as to make the batsman play a drive or cut on the off side.

Top Spin or Flipper

The top spin delivery or flipper is another weapon in the leg spinner's arsenal. This is a delivery which goes straight after pitching or comes slightly into the right-hand batsman. The accomplished leg spinner Narendra Hirwani once told me that it took him years of practice to master the top spin.

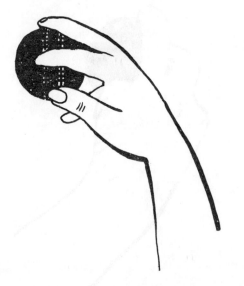

Fig. 5.10 The grip for top spin

Checklist
1. The grip (Fig. 5.10) is almost the same as for leg spin. The difference is that the bowler does not spin the ball; he just pushes it through in a clockwise direction with the first finger.
2. The ball moves quicker in the air and also off the wicket.
3. The run-up for every delivery is identical, and the bowler should try to bowl with as much a side-on action as possible (except for the

googly). He should keep his head steady, with the eyes focussed on the spot where he intends to pitch the ball.

4. The bowler's wrist remains stiff, and the ball is 'floated' towards the batsman. The bowler presses down with his fingers on the ball in a clockwise direction so that the ball goes straight through.

5. The flipper is bowled on, or slightly away from, the off stump, slightly short of length, in order to make the batsman play the cut or pull. This could result in the batsman spooning a catch, or being bowled, or falling victim to lbw (leg before wicket) in case the bowler is adroit enough to hoodwink the batsman!

Before concluding this section, let me emphasise some useful points. Leg spinners must have a loose and flexible wrist, so that they can achieve maximum twist and turn. The spin bowler should 'read' a batsman carefully, thereby judging his strong and weak points, especially the latter so that he can exploit them as and when required. He should constantly check out the fielders' positions and effect changes strategically in consultation with the captain. As the spinner walks up to the start of his run-up, he should plan his next delivery clearly. He should not hesitate to experiment with his bowling techniques if he has the requisite control over line and length.

The wicket-keeper can be an ideal 'guide'. He can tell whether or not a bowler is maintaining a good line and length. He can also assess the flight pattern and the amount of turn a bowler can achieve. Based on the wicket-keeper's observations, a bowler can modify his attack to make it more effective.

One very important factor in spin bowling pertains to *flight*. (See Chapter 2 for a description of flight.) The bowler should flight the ball appreciably in order to achieve various types of spin, which could deceive the batsman. However, on slow wickets, the bowler should push the ball through so that he can get more bite from the wicket.

A spinner should try to maintain the shine on the ball, at least on one side, because other pace bowlers would be operating as well and they need the shine to achieve swing.

Regular practice is absolutely essential for perfecting leg spin; a minimum of two hours every day at the nets is necessary. One should remember that leg spin is one form of bowling from which one cannot afford to take a break!

Off Spin

There have been many outstanding right-hand off spinners in the history of cricket, who have 'spun webs' around batsmen, but I would place E.A.S. Prasanna at the top of the lot. His ability to bowl different kinds of deliveries with the same action is nothing short of phenomenal. His guile and deception are legendary. I have had the good fortune of playing a lot of cricket with and against Prasanna, which proved highly beneficial to me.

I remember one particular India vs. England test match at Bombay, in which Roger Tolchard was going great guns against the Indian spinners. He was dancing down the wicket frequently and walloping the spinners all over the place. At times, he emerged from his crease even before the ball was bowled. Obviously, Prasanna had observed this feature. He kept on bowling normally for a while, but, suddenly, he held back one delivery for a slightly longer period. By that time, Tolchard had already come down the wicket. Prasanna skilfully delivered the ball wide of the leg side and the batsman was out, stumped. I think this was a great piece of bowling, involving both imagination and improvisation.

The other prominent off-spinners who come to my mind include Ghulam Ahmed (India), Lance Gibbs (West Indies), Fred Titmus (England), S. Venkataraghavan (India) and John Emburey (England).

By the way, an off spin delivery is one which, after pitching, comes *into* a right-handed batsman.

Fig. 5. 11 The off spin grip

Grip

For off spin, the first two fingers are spread out as much as possible. The top joints of both these fingers hold the ball across the seam to provide the optimum spinning grip. The ball is spun with the first finger. The third finger and also the thumb act as a support. (See Fig. 5.11.) The ball should be held firmly, but comfortably, so that it does not fall out of the hand. It should be noted that the thumb does not play any part in spinning the ball.

By chance, if a bowler has small fingers and cannot grip the ball across the seam, as an alternative grip, the first finger can be made to lie alongside the seam and the second finger spread apart (as widely as possible), with the thumb resting underneath for support.

Checklist

1. An off spinner doesn't require a very long run-up. However, the distance should be sufficient to provide a good rhythm. The bowler must have a side-on action, i.e., while bowling, he must look over his left shoulder. Such an action would assist in turning the ball appreciably, while bowling to left-handed or right-handed batsman. An off spinner can also bowl with an open chested action but the effect of the spin would be diminished because the bowler would not be able to put much of body action into the delivery.
2. The right arm should come up high and straight.
3. The spinning action is identical to opening a door knob in a clockwise direction; in other words, the finger is rolled along the seam in a clockwise direction.

4. The fingers and the wrist should work together in coordination for optimum effect.
5. The bowler should twist his hips and pivot on his front foot so that he can put in more body action and can spin the ball more.
6. An off spinner's final stride is always small so that he can stand up to his full height to bowl effectively.
7. The bowler should flight the ball while bowling off spin, so as to enable him to deceive the batsman and break through his defences.

The Straight Delivery (or Floater)

As in the case of leg spinners, off spinners also should develop a variation in their bowling. The only other delivery, apart from off spin, that an off spinner can bowl is the straight delivery. This delivery, as the name implies, goes straight after pitching. It is bowled with the same action as the off spin delivery but instead of turning, it moves straight into the batsman, catching him by surprise. Normally, the batsman ends up offering a catch to the slips or to the wicket-keeper. E.A.S. Prasanna was a past master at beguiling batsman convincingly with this delivery, which yielded him a large number of wickets.

Checklist

1. For the straight delivery, some changes in grip are obviously necessary *vis-à-vis* the off break. The ball should be held across the seam but the first finger comes on top of the seam, which should face the third man position at the time of delivery. (See Fig. 5. 12.)
2. The bowler must adopt a side-on action to put in maximum body action (into the delivery). Instead of spinning the ball, the bowler should keep his wrist stiff and float the ball (push it through), keeping in mind that the seam should be facing third man.
3. The bowler should bowl from a spot close to the wicket, pivoting on his front foot and twisting his hips appropriately to move out of the wickets. The bowling arm should be used vigorously, finishing on the outside of the left thigh.
4. The straight delivery is bowled a bit quicker than regular off spin.

There exists an alternative grip for the floater, in which the thumb is placed behind the ball during delivery. In this case, the following points need to be noted:

(1) Instead of spinning the ball, the bowler merely pushes it through towards the slips.
(2) The bowler should let his first finger slide round and under the ball as it leaves the hand.

Fig. 5.12 Grip for the floater

(3) When bowling the straight delivery, the bowler should always keep the shiny part of the ball facing outwards. If the conditions are suitable for swing bowling, the ball would move and swerve in the air like an outswinger. Therefore, to avoid this possibility, it is important that the bowler give some air to the straight delivery.

One cannot become an effective spin bowler by merely using one's fingers. The ultimate result has to be achieved by employing the optimum combination of fingers, wrist, shoulders, hips and the action of pivoting at the required moment.

A bowler must be able to skilfully adapt his bowling techniques according to the nature of the wicket and the atmospheric conditions. Consequently, he must have variety in his attack. He should be able to flight the ball or else push it through quickly, depending on the specific circumstances.

LEFT ARM SPIN

Left arm off spinners have been highly successful because many right-handed batsmen find it difficult to play the leaving ball.

Over the years, India has produced some all-time great left arm spinners. Who can forget the superb Vinoo Mankad or the ever consistent Bishen Singh Bedi? Mankad's magical bowling spells helped India notch up several victories. Bedi's majestic but effortless run-up, action and flight are still imprinted in my memory. He broke through the defence of many batsmen — even seasoned players — with his remarkable guile and subtle variation.

Other left arm Indian spinners who have made a distinct mark include Dilip Doshi, Maninder Singh and Ravi Shastri. There were some other fine left arm spinners such as Rajinder Goel and P. Shivalkar but, unfortunately, they could not play in any test match because Bedi had established himself very firmly in the saddle. I am sure had the two aforementioned spinners belonged to a different time frame, they would have emerged as successful as Mankad or Bedi!

A left arm off spin delivery is one which, after pitching, turns towards the slips (i.e., leg to off for a right handed batsman). The left arm off spinner bowls in the same manner as a right-hand off spinner. If a right-hand batsman is facing, then the left arm off spin becomes leg spin to him, that is, the ball tends to leave the bat after pitching.

Most of the slow left arm spinners tend to bowl round the wicket to right-handed batsman in order to get a better angle so that the ball could come in with the arm and then spin the other way.

Grip

The grip is exactly like that for the right-hand off spin, the only difference is that the ball is held in the left hand, with the first two fingers across the seam. The third finger and the thumb support the ball. The ball should be held between the first two fingers in a sufficiently tight manner so that even if one hits it with the other hand, it does not get dislodged.

Checklist
1. The first finger plays an important part in spinning the ball. The entire pressure falls on the first finger. It is as if one were closing a door knob (in the anti-clockwise direction). The first finger should be in the line of the second finger. As already mentioned, the second finger and the thumb play a 'supporting role'.
2. As mentioned earlier, most left arm spinners tend to bowl round the wicket. While doing so, many of them run in between the umpire and the stumps and maintain a side-on position in order to put more body action into the delivery.
3. The run-up should be short and smooth. The bowler should keep looking over his right shoulder to determine the spot where he intends to pitch the ball. The final stride should be small.
4. Ideally, at the time of delivery, the left toe should be parallel to the bowling crease and the right toe should point towards the slips.
5. The bowler's left arm should come high and straight just before releasing the ball.
6. At the time of delivery, the bowler should pivot on his front foot, twist his hips and bring down his bowling arm vigorously, taking his right arm high. He should use full body action to spin the ball across to the right-handed batsman. His follow through should be smooth and easy.

Arm Ball or Armer

A competent left arm bowler should be proficient in bowling the 'arm ball' or 'armer'. Invariably, right-handed batsmen tend to spoon a catch close to the wickets or are bowled when they try to cut an armer, which comes slightly into the batsman. I remember a match in Australia in 1977, in which Bedi's bowling was punished severely by Kim Hughes in one particular over. The first three balls were hammered by Hughes to the boundary. The fourth ball was a lovely armer deftly slipped in by Bedi. This delivery uprooted Hughes' stumps as he stepped back to play the square cut. The armer can provide a good haul of wickets, if bowled properly.

Grip

A slight change in grip is needed for the armer. The ball is held across the seam but, in this case, the first finger is placed on top of the seam. At the time of delivery, the seam should be facing the fine leg position, when bowling to a right-handed batsman.

Checklist

1. When an armer is bowled, the entire pressure is on the first finger.
2. At the time of delivery, the bowler's wrist should remain stiff. He should just 'float' the ball straight on, so that it can land on the seam and come in to the right-handed batsman.
3. The armer is bowled slightly faster than conventional left arm spin, so that it comes in quicker, after pitching, to the batsman.
4. The bowler should maintain a side-on action at the time of delivery.
5. When delivering the ball, the bowler's arm should ideally be straight. After the action is complete, the bowling arm should finish in front of the thigh of the front (right) leg.
6. The armer should ideally be bowled from the edge of the crease so that the bowler can get a better angle. Also, if there is a breeze blowing in a suitable direction, it could be used to assist in making the ball move in the air and come in more after pitching.
7. On the basis of my experience, I can state that if the armer is bowled with a slightly round arm action, it comes in more to the right-handed batsman. Two gifted left arm spinners, namely, Rajinder Goel and P. Shivalkar (mentioned earlier) used to bowl the armer with a slightly roundish arm with maximum success.

The Chinaman

The chinaman can be termed as the 'left arm leg spin' — another useful variation. The grip is similar to that of a right-handed leg spinner but *with the left hand*. A chinaman comes into a right-hand batsman like off spin. And when the left arm spinner bowls a googly, it becomes *leg spin* for a right-hand batsman and leaves him.

BOWLING ACCORDING TO THE WICKETS

A bowler should always remember to bowl *according to the nature of the wicket*; in other words, he should put the wicket to optimum use. For instance, if a wicket is turning, the bowler should maintain a good line and length, and take maximum advantage of the assistance offered by the wicket. He should *not* try 'experiments' with his bowling, which could prove counterproductive. Let me cite an example in this context. In the 1987-88 series, when we were playing against Pakistan at Bangalore on a real turning wicket, where it was difficult to even bowl a straight ball, Pakistan managed to win the match by bowling accurately and exploiting the pitch to the maximum extent, without trying any 'experiments'. On the contrary, our bowlers conceded too many runs with their 'experimental' bowling.

On a wicket favouring the spin bowlers, they must do everything possible to get the batsmen out as quickly as possible. Flight plays an important role in deceiving a batsman, because he could spoon up a catch by playing his stroke too early as he expects the ball to be a half volley, whereas it suddenly dips in, resulting in a mishit. Several bowlers including Jim Laker, Lance Gibbs, B.S. Bedi, E.A.S. Prasanna, B. S. Chandrashekhar and Abdul Qadir were remarkable craftsmen of spin bowling and, on good wickets, their performance proved exceptionally brilliant.

OTHER IMPORTANT POINTS TO BE REMEMBERED

1. A bowler should wear spiked shoes in order to achieve the maximum grip.
2. A bowler must develop a smooth follow through and should be ever ready to field to his own bowling.
3. A bowler should constantly concentrate on the batsman's *grip* and accordingly vary his delivery so as to exploit the batsman's weak points. For instance:
   (a) If a batsman holds the bat at the top with both hands together, this indicates that he intends to drive the ball.
   (b) However, if there is a large gap between the two hands, i.e., the left hand holding the bat at the top and right hand at the bottom, and the handle is clearly visible, this shows that the batsman is a strong back foot player and would opt for cuts and pull shots.
4. The bowler should keep his chin high (as if he were trying to read the inscription on the ball) so that he can flight the ball well and then dip it into the batsman.

A QUICK SUMMING UP

Let me briefly sum up the various deliveries bowled by right arm bowlers to right-handed batsmen and how they 'behave':

1. *Outswinger:* This moves in the air from leg to off and leaves the batsman.

2. *Inswinger:* This moves in the air from off to leg and comes into the batsman.

3. *Off cutter:* This comes into the batsman after pitching (off to leg).

4. *Leg cutter:* This leaves the batsman after pitching (leg to off) and goes towards the slips.

5. *Leg spin/break:* After pitching, the ball turns from leg to off.

6. *Googly:* After pitching, the ball comes into the batsman from off to leg.

7. *Flipper:* This goes straight after pitching.

8. *Off spin:* This turns and comes into the batsman from off to leg, after pitching.

9. *Straight ball:* After pitching, this goes straight or moves slightly away from the batsman.

Let me now move on to a left arm bowler bowling to a right-handed batsman. In this category, we have the following:

1. *Left arm off spin:* After pitching, this goes from leg to off.

2. *Arm ball or armer:* This comes in slightly, or goes straight, to the batsman.

3. *Chinaman:* This comes in to the right-hand batsman after pitching; a chinaman googly goes from leg to off.

ROUNDING OFF
Finally, let me point out that certain exercises prove useful in strengthening a spin bowler's fingers, wrist and forearms. For instance, Ravi Shastri's methods are as follows: Take a tennis ball or squash ball and squeeze it with your fingers to the extent possible. For the wrists, take a wet towel and try to wring it to the extent possible.

Let me re-emphasise a few important points with respect to bowling:

1. Bowling involves a good deal of strenuous activity. To attain perfection in this skill, one must practise for at least two hours a day, sincerely and purposefully.

2. For practising bowling, in case a bowler cannot 'entice' a batsman to play his deliveries, he should at least find a wicket-keeper (to catch or retrieve the ball for him). If even this is not possible, then he can bowl against a wall. He should mark the good length spot on the wicket and try to repeatedly pitch his deliveries on them (again, regular practice is needed).

3. Natural talent is always useful, but practice makes it perfect.

I would like to once again dwell upon the vital importance of having a good amount of variation in one's bowling attack. Variation is essential in order to disturb the concentration of a batsman. All great fast and slow bowlers possess an array of different types of deliveries to baffle the batsman. Let me give examples to reinforce my statement. Andy Roberts could bowl both slow and fast bouncers. Kapil Dev could bowl similar types of deliveries with different speeds. Sir Richard Hadlee could surprise the batsman with his 'express deliveries'. Imran Khan's 'bag of tricks' included the 'banana swing'. Joel Garner was proficient in delivering the 'perfect yorker' and Michael Holding could bowl quick ones with a shortened run-up with equal ease.

A bowler should always keep in mind the fact that stereotyped and unimaginative bowling becomes very easy to play. A bowler should make optimum use of the bowling crease to achieve variation in his attack. E.A.S. Prasanna, sometimes, used to bowl from behind the bowling crease in order to perplex the batsman. B.S. Bedi used to flabbergast the batsmen with subtle variations in flight and Chandrashekhar could leave batsmen floundering and bewildered by his faster delivery, which used to be quicker than that of an Indian medium pacer!

Six

Field Placement for Different Types of Bowling

Field placement plays a very important role in a team's success. In fact, this factor could sometimes mean the crucial difference between victory and defeat, especially in one-day matches. Precise field placement calls for a great deal of experience and knowledge on the part of both the bowler and the captain. In combination, they place the fielders in correct positions in order to stop runs from being scored and also snap up catches. Both should have a good knowledge of the wickets and the effect of atmospheric conditions on them. They should also be able to identify and exploit the weaknesses of the opposing team's batsmen. They must know when exactly to set an attacking field and when a defensive field. Above all, the bowler and the captain must have excellent rapport so that they can plan their strategy and tactics properly.

FIELD PLACING FOR FAST/MEDIUM PACE BOWLING

For Outswing

I was fortunate enough to play with or against top-class swing bowlers such as Kapil Dev, Sir Richard Hadlee, Ian Botham and Imran Khan. Each one of them had his own incisive form of attack and each could really swing the ball formidably. They altered their field placements according to the nature of the wicket, the atmospheric conditions and the exigent demands of the situation. One must always remember the basic rule that, nowadays, one cannot have more than two fielders behind square leg. During the good old days of body line bowling, under the captaincy of England's Douglas Jardine, one could place as many fielders as one liked on the leg side. Keeping in view one's intended line of attack, one must accordingly chalk out the field placement in consultation with the captain. Most pace bowlers tend to bowl on the off stump or slightly outside. Consequently they set their field accordingly.

As stated in the previous chapter, an outswing delivery is one which leaves the bat, i.e., it moves towards the off side slips from the leg side. Therefore, most catches would come to the slips. Consequently to begin with, three slips, a gully and a cover point are needed.

Also, a widish mid-off is needed (i.e., positioned between extra covers and orthodox mid-off). If the wicket favours pace and bounce, the cover point fielder can be placed finer as also the gully fielder. On the other hand, if the wicket is slow, the gully can move a bit squarer. No batsman in the world, however proficient and renowned he may be, is completely sure of himself at the start of his innings. Therefore, it is not only useful but also necessary to attack by bowling right up to the batsman, especially when the ball is new and can swing considerably. Depending on the situation and atmospheric conditions, a fourth slip can also be stationed (instead of mid-off). (See Fig. 6.1.)

After some time, one slip can be moved to the third man position. Also, initially, a forward short leg would be needed, who can later take up position at square leg or else between mid-wicket and mid-on. When the ball is swinging a great deal, in the line of the off stump or just outside, a bowler does not need too many fielders on the leg side. A three-six (leg-off) combination would be ideal.

For Inswing

As already stated, the inswinger is a delivery which comes into a right-handed batsman, i.e., it moves from the off stump or slightly outside the off stump to the leg side. Initially, the field placement could comprise three slips, although two slips and a widish gully are more than enough. (See Fig. 6.2.) In this context, let me recount the field placement employed by Imran Khan, who was an outstanding inswing bowler. He would start with three slips, gully, cover point, mid-off, fine leg, leg gully or forward short leg and silly mid-on. After a few overs had been bowled, when the batsman usually becomes 'set', the third slip was moved to the third man position; the silly mid-on to mid-on and the forward short leg to square leg (near the umpire). However, if the bowlers could still swing the ball, the forward short leg fielder was retained.

It is important to note when *a left arm inswing medium pacer* is bowling over the wicket and angling the ball across the right-handed batsman, the field placing should be identical to that for a *right arm outswing bowler*. Similarly, when a *left arm outswing bowler* is operating, the field placement should be identical to that for a *right arm inswing bowler*. However, the wicket-keeper and the slips should stand slightly squarer (wider) on the off side so as to enable them to see the bowler clearly.

FIELD PLACEMENT FOR DEFENSIVE BOWLING

The purpose behind defensive bowling is to halt or check the flow of runs. In such a situation, the bowlers are not really trying to get the batsmen out. However, if they manage to dismiss them, this proves to be a bonus. The bowlers attempt to bowl straight and slightly short of a length, so that the batsman is unable to play his strokes freely.

Defensive bowling usually becomes necessary when the two batsmen at the centre have become properly 'set' and have amassed a huge score. Moreover, such bowling is resorted to when there is nothing in the wicket to assist the bowlers and the runs flow freely. Consequently, the field placement is altered so that the fielders move from catching

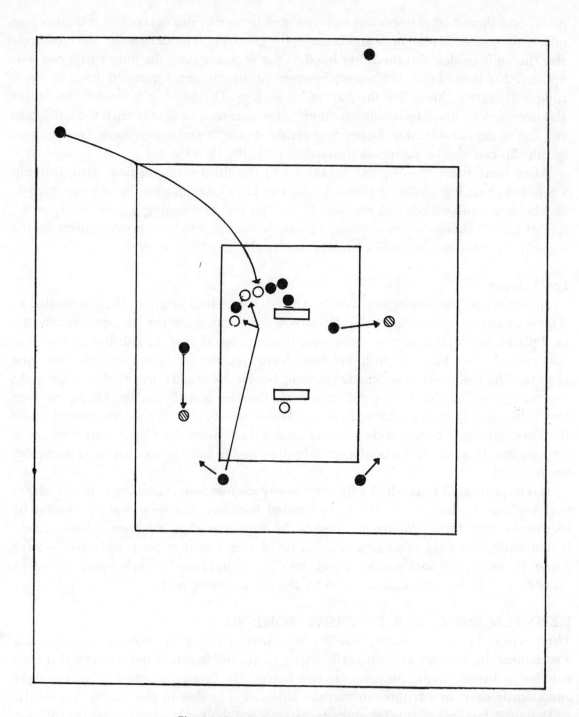

Fig. 6.1 Sample field placement for outswing

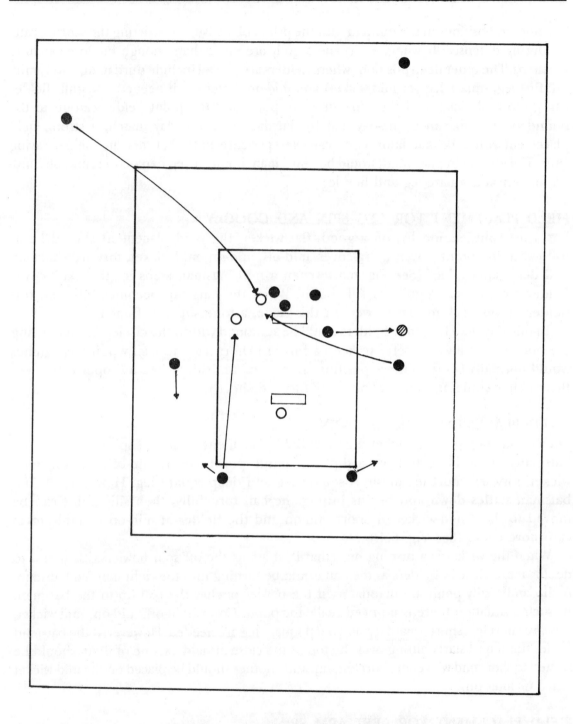

Fig. 6.2 Sample field placement for inswing

positions to positions in the outfield with the prime objective of restricting the scoring rate.

During defensive bowling, a slip and a gully are more than enough in close catching positions. The other deep positions where fielders are placed include third man, cover, mid-off, fine leg, square leg (or mid-wicket) and mid-on. Later on, if needed, the gully fielder can go to mid-wicket and the slip can go to point and the point fielder can go to the boundary (just like in a one-day match). Further, in a one-day match, a strong field placement within the mandatory circle can exert pressure on the batsmen and help in saving runs. The ideal field placement would be: third man, point, cover, extra-cover, mid-off, mid-on, mid-wicket, square leg and fine leg.

FIELD PLACEMENT FOR LEG SPIN AND GOOGLY

For a leg spinner, ideally, on a good, flat wicket, the field placement should be as follows: a slip, point, cover, extra-cover, mid-off, mid-on, mid-wicket, forward short leg and deep square leg. (See Fig. 6.3.) When a new batsman steps in, the extra-cover fielder moves over to gully or silly point. When the batsman becomes fully set, this fielder moves back to extra-cover. At this stage, a lone slip is sufficient.

In one-day matches, four fielders could be stationed within the circle. When bowling the googly, it is always useful to keep a forward short leg and a silly point as catches would normally come to these positions in case of a mishit. When a flipper is bowled, the catches come at slip, silly point or forward short leg.

FIELD PLACEMENT FOR OFF SPIN

On a good, easy playing wicket the ideal field placement for an off spinner (for a new batsman) would be as follows: a slip, silly point, point, cover, mid-off, mid-on, mid-wicket, forward short leg or short square leg and deep square leg. However, when a batsman settles down and begins hitting the ball forcefully, then silly point can be moved to short mid-wicket or short mid-on and the fielder at mid-on or mid-wicket can move back. (See Fig. 6.4.)

When the wicket is a turning one, that is, it assists the off spin bowlers, it's useful to deploy more close-in fielders as the ball would be turning into the right-handed batsman. A slip and a silly point are mandatory if the bowler pitches the ball up to the batsman. In such a situation there is no need really for point. Cover, mid-off, mid-on, mid-wicket, forward short leg, short square leg and deep square leg are needed. However, if the batsman settles down and starts hitting over the top of the close-in fielders, one of them should be shifted to short mid-wicket or short mid-on, and another should be placed on the mid-wicket fence or long on.

FIELD PLACEMENT FOR LEFT ARM SPIN

On a good and stable wicket, the initial field placement for a left arm spinner would be as follows: slip, silly point, point, cover, mid-off, mid-on, mid-wicket, forward short leg and deep square leg. Later on, the silly point can move to extra cover and the

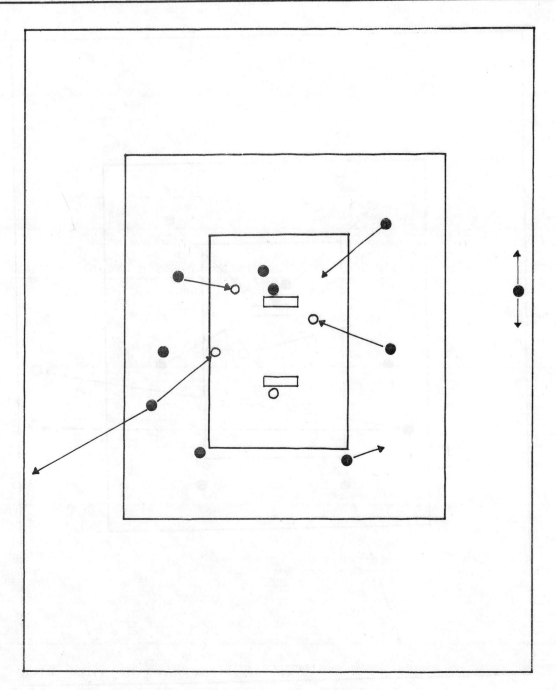

Fig. 6.3 Sample field placement for leg spin/googly

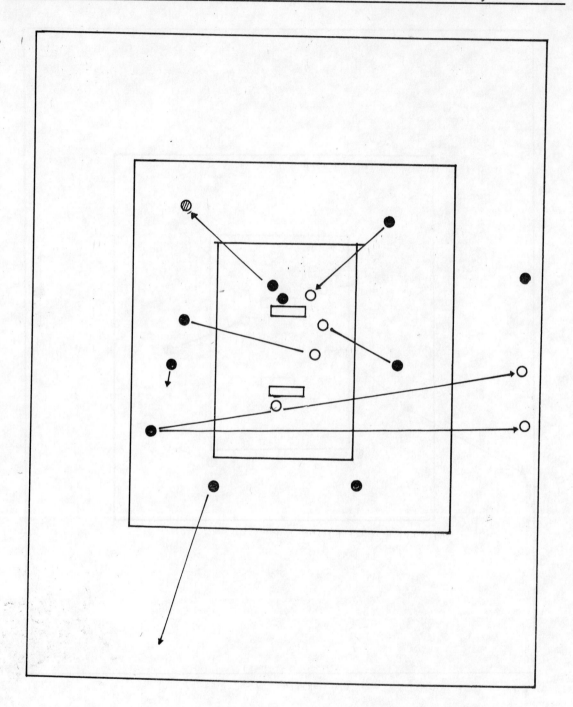

Fig. 6.4 Sample field placement for off spin

forward short leg can shift to silly point, depending on the specific situation.

On a turning wicket, the field placement requires certain alterations. In this case, it should be initially as follows: Slip, gully, silly point, forward short leg, point, cover, mid-off, mid-on and square leg. However, once the batsman gets set, silly point or gully can move over to mid-wicket, depending on the specific situation. The fielders should be placed in deep positions only if the batsman is consistently hitting the ball over the top of the close-in fielders.

Seven
The Importance of Wicket-Keeping

The wicket-keeper's job is a very difficult, but vital, one, because he is virtually at the centre of all the action taking place on the field. He has to concentrate on each and every delivery, and accordingly adjust his position and modify his tactics. He has to be extremely agile and alert and should possess lightning reflexes. An energetic and inspiring wicket-keeper can boost the morale of the entire team. Since he is at a vantage point to observe the batsmen, he can offer valuable tips to the bowlers and fielders about how to get them out.

I feel that wicket-keepers are born and not made. Invariably, all great wicket-keepers have been short in stature, such as Bert Oldfield, Allan Knott, Rodney Marsh, Wasim Bari, Syed Kirmani, Kiran More and Bob Taylor. I once questioned Kiran More as to why this was so. He replied that short players found it easy to bend and collect the ball easily. If one is tall, then frequent bending could affect the back and may lead to assorted pulls and aches.

A wicket-keeper's task is a thankless one, as it is felt that because he wears gloves and pads (i.e., he is well protected) he cannot afford to miss any catch or let the ball go past him. Even if he lets an extra run go by, despite having saved numerous others, it appears as if all his efforts have been wasted. A bad keeper can become a liability to the team, especially if he drops catches or misfields during crucial stages of the game. However, a good keeper can always come back into the game, and exhibit an amazing performance, and, in the process, enjoy himself.

A born wicket-keeper has a natural ability to latch on to the ball, when standing up to either a pace bowler or a spinner. Smooth mobility and quick reflexes can be acquired with constant practice and intense exercise. Physical fitness plays a vital role in any wicket-keeper's performance. Also, a keen sense of humour can relieve the tension on the field and pep up his teammates' confidence.

EQUIPMENT FOR WICKET-KEEPERS
The wicket-keeper's job is undeniably a challenging and dangerous one, as he is

constantly exposed to the bowling. Also, he usually stands close to the batsman while doing his job. A wicket-keeper can be compared to a batsman; the only difference is that the batsman is in front of the wicket and holding a bat and the keeper is behind the wickets, wearing thick and heavy gloves.

The gloves form the most important equipment for the wicket-keeper. A pair of gloves could prove to be the make-or-break factor! Gloves can elevate the wicket-keeper to test status or else reduce him to club level. Consequently, he should choose his gloves carefully and maintain them in excellent condition. An ideal pair of leather gloves should be comfortably loose, but not too loose, and also the inner gloves (usually made of cotton) should fit snugly. A keeper should be able to take off the gloves easily as and when required. He should 'season' his gloves so that they can fit properly and he can hold the ball safely and comfortably. Here are a few tips for making a new pair of gloves more useful:

1. The palms of the new gloves should be hammered lightly with the bottom of a cricket bat to a cup-like form for catching purposes. Such a form can also be obtained by taking a lot of short catches (through deliberate practice).
2. The surface of the gloves should have soft, pimpled rubber. In case the surface gets worn out (becomes smooth) it should be replaced immediately, otherwise the keeper will face problems while catching the ball.
3. While collecting the ball, the keeper must be able to feel the ball in his palm. Therefore, too much padding should not be used in the palm of the glove.
4. Ideally, the gloves should be light so as to enable quick movement of the arms.
5. The inner gloves also form part of the 'gloves equipment'. The inner gloves are usually made of chamois leather or cotton. Both kinds are equally effective. The inner gloves must have elastic bands at the top, which are not too tight so as to cause discomfort. This will enable the keeper to remove the main outer gloves easily. The inner gloves are wetted frequently in order to remove their stiffness, which results due to perspiration.

The other important equipment of a keeper pertains to his footwear. Most keepers opt for rubber boots, which enable them to move freely and easily. If the boots are studded with spikes, it should be ensured that the spikes are not too long as they tend to get stuck in the wicket while moving or pivoting. Such an impediment can cause injuries to the ankles and knees. Also, a keeper should wear a suitable headgear to protect him from the heat and glare and enable him to focus properly on the ball. A keeper should wear light, but sturdy and protective, pads which should make him feel comfortable without hampering his movement in any way. Last but not the least, a very essential item is the abdominal guard which every keeper must wear.

WICKET-KEEPING STANCE

Before a keeper takes his stance, he should draw an imaginary line behind the off stump in order to position his left foot properly, while standing up to the wickets, to a slow bowler. When he squats, he should make sure that both his hands touch the wickets easily. The best way of ensuring this is to just touch the leg stump with the left hand and the off stump with the right hand.

One must have seen wicket-keepers adopting two different stances, namely (a) standing with hands cupped in front and (b) squatting position with the fingertips (i.e., glove tips) just touching the ground with the palms facing the wickets (or facing inwards). (See Fig. 7.1)

Fig. 7.1 A typical stance of a wicket-keeper

Most wicket-keepers prefer the squatting position as the body weight is equally distributed on the balls of both feet, which are placed comfortably apart. The knees are well bent, and the hands are close together, resting between the legs. As just stated, the glove tips just touch the ground and the palms face the wickets (or the bowler). The chin is kept well up from the chest and the eyes are kept focussed first on the bowler's hand and then on the batsman's blade and the ball. The eyes should be level at one specific angle.

POSITION OF THE KEEPER

A wicket-keeper should position himself depending upon the type of bowling. For instance, if a fast bowler is operating, the wicket-keeper usually stands a few metres behind the wickets. On the other hand, if a spinner or a medium pacer is in action, the keeper normally stands up to the wickets.

Standing up to the wicket is one of the most demanding tasks that a keeper has to perform. He has to be quick on his feet, with lightning reflexes. The position of the inside foot (left) should be in the line of the off stump so that the keeper can get a clear view of the bowler's arm.

Fig. 7.2 Collecting while standing back

When standing back also (see Fig. 7.2), the keeper must have a clear view of the bowler's arm and the trajectory of the ball. He should not position himself too wide off the off stump because this will create problems while reaching for deliveries outside the leg stump. The precise position a keeper should take up would depend upon factors such as whether a pace bowler or a spinner is operating (left arm or right arm) and also the pace and bounce of the wicket and the atmospheric conditions.

A common error that keepers commit with respect to their position is that they stand in 'no man's land', i.e., either too far from, or too close to, the wicket. If a keeper stands too far back, there is a distinct possibility that he may drop a catch (being too far away), resulting from a snick. If he stands too close, there is the danger of getting hurt, sometimes seriously. Consequently, he should choose the ideal position, where he can collect the ball easily and comfortably, normally between knee to waist height. Ideally, the keeper should collect the ball with his hands forward as its trajectory drops.

Once a keeper has positioned himself properly and adopted a stance, he should *presume* that every ball will come to him whether or not the batsman makes contact with the ball.

Here are a few guidelines for prospective keepers (see also Fig. 7.3):

1. The wicket-keeper should always concentrate on the bowler's hand so that he can ascertain what kind of delivery to expect.
2. The keeper should first carefully pick up the flight and line of the ball and only then get up along with the bounce of the delivery.
3. The keeper should get behind the line of the ball, but should be ready to move out of the line in case of a short delivery. Such readiness would enable him to get into position

Fig. 7.3 Collecting on the off side

quickly if the ball bounces awkwardly or if it keeps low.

4. The ball should always be collected with the arms kept straight, but relaxed with the elbows bent.

5. The keeper should ascertain the trajectory of the delivery and accordingly move quickly into position but should be ready for any split-second deviations.

6. Many keepers tend to place their outside (right) foot back when collecting a ball which bounces awkwardly. I feel that this method is suitable provided the keeper's hands can quickly reach the wickets, if required.

7. The keeper should rest his body weight on the foot closer to the wicket and slightly tilt his body towards the wickets. This is because as soon as he has the ball in his hand, he can instantly break the wickets, if the occasion so demands.

8. The small finger of the keeper's strong hand should remain on top of the small finger of the other hand so that both hands can make a big cup in order to collect the ball easily.

9. It becomes very difficult and awkward for the keeper to collect or catch the ball if a batsman plays off the back foot. Therefore, he should try to gather the ball as close to the body as possible.

10. As far as possible, the keeper should anticipate the trajectory of the ball and position himself to receive it rather than try to snatch it. He should close his hands securely around the ball, collecting it in the strong hand as far as possible.

11. A keeper should keep his head down with his eyes focussed on the ball so that he can collect it comfortably. He should leap or dive only if the ball bounces a great deal so as to catch hold of it. After getting hold of the ball (if not for a catch), the keeper should move very quickly towards the wickets to stump the batsman, if the opportunity arises.

12. The keeper should try to collect the ball in the line of the right leg. If by chance, even if he misses the ball, it should hit his right leg and stop.

COLLECTING THE BALL ON THE LEG SIDE

Collecting on the leg side has invariably proved to be a difficult proposition for wicket-keepers. This is because when a keeper is standing up to the wickets, he loses sight of the ball momentarily if it moves to the leg side as his view is blocked by the batsman. For leg side collection, here are a few points to be remembered:

1. The keeper should move to the leg side only after the ball has pitched and its trajectory is towards the leg side.

2. The keeper should move a bit late but quickly.

3. When a keeper attempts to gather a leg side delivery, he should take his left foot as far as possible to his left and then move the right foot towards the left foot, collecting the ball with his strong hand, preferably. To the extent possible, he should keep his eyes on the ball, with the hand down and the elbows free from

Fig. 7.4 Collecting on the leg side

the body so that he can utilise his hands swiftly. (See Fig. 7.4.)

WICKET-KEEPING WHEN STANDING BACK

As already stated, a keeper usually stands back to medium pacers and fast bowlers. At the point at which he decides to stand, he should make a mark.

While collecting deliveries that come below chest height, the keeper's palms should face the bowler, with the fingers pointing downwards. But for higher level deliveries, the keeper normally collects them with the strong hand, with the palm facing the bowler but the fingers pointing upward. The other hand plays a supporting role.

THE IMPORTANCE OF CONCENTRATION

Concentration is the key factor in wicket-keeping. While a batsman at the non-striker's end or some fielders can afford to relax their concentration, a wicket-keeper just cannot do so. The moment he loses his concentration, he inevitably drops the ball or fumbles with it. The ideal way to maintain one's concentration is from session to session. Keepers tend to focus on the coming breaks such as lunch break or tea break and tend to lose their concentration. Instead, they should work harder on concentrating just before such breaks and relax during the breaks as much as possible.

SUMMING UP

From the foregoing discussion, it is evident that wicket-keeping demands a lot of hard work and effort. Constant practice and physical exercises are absolutely essential. Side running should be practised extensively. Constant stretching of muscles is very important in order to make the body flexible and supple. Altertness and quick reflexes can make all the difference between winning and losing.

Net practice is absolutely essential. A keeper should keep wickets for at least eight different batsmen at the nets as seriously as while playing in a match.

Here are a few more points which wicket-keepers would do well to remember:

1. A keeper should always try to collect the ball with his strong hand. He should avoid using the pads to stop the ball, except as a last resort.
2. The wicket-keeper occupies a vantage position in the field and is the best judge of the game. He can apprise the captain about the various bowlers' abilities and

weaknesses, whether they have lost their 'fire' or not. He can also identify the strong and weak points of the rival team's batsmen and inform his captain accordingly.

3.   The keeper also serves as an extra fielder. Whenever the batsmen attempt a cheeky single he can try to pick up the ball and break the wickets. While hurling the ball, he should take off the glove from the throwing hand.

4.   A good keeper always makes a bad throw from a fielder look good. He should always stay at striking distance from the stumps when collecting throws. As far as possible the throws should be collected behind the stumps in order to effect run outs, which are normally split-second activities.

5.   While standing back, the keeper should rush forward as soon as the batsman has played his stroke (in case the ball is not coming to him) in order to collect the throw from a fielder. He should always expect fielders to throw the ball back and should instinctively move his hand towards the wickets.

6.   The game of squash proves an ideal one to keep a wicket-keeper fit and active and hone his reflexes to perfection.

7.   A wicket-keeper should practise regularly and sincerely at that. He should collect the ball from different angles (hurled towards him by the fielders) including awkward and difficult positions. He should practise holding on to catches on all sides.

8.   For improving his reflexes a keeper should sit against a wall and ask someone to throw the ball from behind. He should then attempt to pick up the ball on the first bounce itself.

9.   The keeper can ask two of his teammates to help him. One of them should hurl the ball from a short distance and the other should take on the role of a batsman who plays only off the front foot. Only a single stump needs to be used. The keeper should practise collecting the ball whenever the batsman misses. More often than not, the batsman will miss the ball rather than middle it.

Finally, by observing the techniques of outstanding wicket-keepers such as Rodney Marsh, Allan Knott, Jeff Dujon, Farookh Engineer, Bob Taylor and Syed Kirmani, one can pick up valuable guidelines and improve one's keeping considerably.

Eight
Captaincy

Cricket is a game in which confidence plays a very important, if not crucial, part. Every player, whether a batsman or a bowler, should possess this quality and should have faith in his own abilities. Cricket can be compared to a game of chess, in which one has to constantly read the opponent's mind and anticipate his strategy and accordingly plan a counterstrategy. One should never underestimate one's own talent, and, at the same time, should not be overwhelmed or cowed down by the name and fame of the opponent, however formidable he may be. One should remember that while competing on the field, it is on a one-to-one basis; therefore, why should a player imagine himself to be inferior or unworthy? However, no player should take the opposition lightly or casually and become overconfident. A captain should explain all these points lucidly to each and every player, so that the entire team approaches the game in a positive frame of mind.

In my opinion, captaincy is always an inborn trait. It does not necessarily follow that all good players are good captains. A good captain is one who can turn a losing game into a winning match, by providing the required guidance, motivation, pep and grit. Obviously, a captain cannot win a match by himself but requires the support of the other players in ensuring success.

Let me cite specific examples to underscore my contentions. Mike Brearly has been rated as one of the best English captains. I am not disputing this point but only stating that it was his other teammates who enabled him to achieve success as a captain. When England beat Australia in the famous Headingly test in the 1980-81 series, after being forced to follow on, it was Ian Botham who played the match of his life, and it was Bob Willis who skittled the Australian batting with his fiery spells of bowling. Of course, it was Brearly who chalked out the strategy regarding bowling changes and field placement and implemented the tactics, which led to victory ultimately.

Another instance of an outstanding captain, who led by example, is that of Pakistan's Imran Khan. By leading from the front, Imran bolstered the entire team's morale and got the best out of his players. During his playing days, Imran was not only a great cricketer but also possessed a keen eye for discovering new talent.

Several present-day Pakistani cricketers, especially Wasim Akram and Waqar Younis, are Imran's protégés, who have now matured into seasoned players. Imran picked up Akram and Younis when they were virtually unknown and developed them into match-winning players in their own individual ways.

In case the reader is wondering as to why I frequently refer to Imran Khan, this is because, throughout his career, he had led from the front and set an outstanding example for his teammates to emulate. He always performed at cent per cent level, and no one could ever question his commitment and zeal. Above all, he kept his team's interest uppermost in his mind. Let me cite an example to prove my statement. Although Abdul Qadir had established himself as one of the outstanding leg spinners against all countries, except India, Imran dropped him from the team after the first test in the 1987-88 series played in India. This was because Imran realised that Qadir would be ineffective against Indian batsmen, who could play spin bowling very well.

Ideally, the captain must be assured of a permanent place in the team. Otherwise, the uncertainty and doubt thus created in his mind could considerably detract from his performing at optimum level. He should be liked and respected by all players both on and off the field. A good captain *earns* the respect and affection of his teammates by proving his abilities on the field, and not by merely demanding them.

In this context, I am reminded once again of the example set by Imran Khan during the Pakistani tour of England in 1987-88. Imran was a bit concerned whether or not his young teammates would prove successful; nevertheless, he used to pep up their morale by praising them extensively and expecting high standards of play from each one of them. And all of them lived up to their captain's expectations. Moreover, on the field, Imran put in inspired performances in all three departments of the game — bowling, batting and fielding. He bowled intelligently and batted with grit and determination, playing some crucial innings. He also snapped up some acrobatic catches. Thus, Imran always led by practical performance and not by mere theoretical planning.

On the other hand, during my 20 years of playing international-level cricket, I have not come across many Indian captains praising their teammates for their performance on the field.

Let us now discuss some other important characteristics a good captain should possess. He should have a good knowledge about the wicket and should be able to ascertain its behaviour; for instance, whether it would help spinners or medium pacers or whether it is a lifeless wicket. He should be able to decide instantly whether to bat first or send in the rival team for batting. Such abilities and perceptions can be acquired only through experience.

A competent captain should be able to judge the calibre of a batsman by carefully studying his grip, stance and back lift. He can then place the fielders accordingly, and ask the bowler to deliver a particular kind of ball which would get the batsman out. Again, I recall, inevitably, the example of Imran Khan who could read the wicket and the conditions proficiently, and adapt immediately to the circumstances. Once, when the Pakistanis were touring India in 1988, their bowlers were finding it difficult to bowl well because of the nature of the wickets. He immediately sent for Iqbal Qasim on an 'SOS' basis, realising that his ace spinner Abdul Qadir was not proving successful. Qasim fulfilled his captain's hopes by playing a vital role in Pakistan's victory in the final test with his accurate left arm spin. A dedicated and committed captain thus ensures that the ultimate goal of victory is reached and does not pay too much attention to any individual's records or achievements, however prominent or famous he may be.

A captain should constantly bolster the morale of his teammates, especially that of the youngsters, by working harder than the others, especially during training sessions. During such sessions, Imran used to bowl and bat longer than his teammates to inspire them and bring out their best.

A captain should possess excellent communication abilities; chiefly a good command over the language, which need not be English but one which enables easy and smooth two-way exchange of thoughts, ideas and decisions. Moreover, a captain must have a keen sense of humour so that he can make the other players relax under pressure and not commit silly mistakes as a result of keyed-up tension.

As already stated, a captain should be liked and respected by his teammates. They should be proud of their captain. In attaining such a position, a captain's behaviour plays a crucial role. He should be unselfish and impartial, but helpful and tactful. He should be willing to share his valuable knowledge with other teammates. He should be caring and sincerely concerned about his players' welfare.

One factor which is absolutely essential is discipline, for both senior and junior players, and it is the captain's job to ensure that discipline is maintained under all circumstances and at all stages. The captain must ensure that no player exhibits bad sportsmanship on the field, such as using abusive language or making offensive gestures, whatever be the provocation. The captain should not hesitate to take the offending player to task in front of his teammates in case repeated warnings in private have proved ineffective. Such instances occur when some players feel that they are indispensable and can behave as they like. However, if a player drops a catch, despite his best efforts, he should not be given a tongue-lashing but encouraged to do better the next time.

A professional captain has to do a good deal of 'homework' with respect to pre-match planning. The captain should conduct a 'brainstorming' session along with his teammates in order that new ideas can be thrown up, new strategies evolved and new tactics planned.

The winning of the toss by a particular captain greatly influences the course of a match. As already mentioned, depending on the nature of the wicket and the atmospheric conditions, a captain should be able to decide, almost instantly, whether to bat first or bowl first. If in doubt after winning the toss, the best course for a captain would be to opt for batting first. Cricket is a funny game. Sometimes, a captain might win the toss but his team may lose the match or vice versa!

The captain has to remain alert and vigilant throughout the match, which is indeed extremely demanding. He has to keep a constant eye not only on the batsmen but also on his own fielders. The fielders should also maintain eye contact with the captain between deliveries in case he decides to effect any field placement changes.

A competent and effective captain employs his bowlers judiciously, especially fast bowlers, taking care to never overuse them or make them feel exhausted. Sometimes, on a helpful wicket, a captain tends to overbowl a particular star pace bowler in his first spell, leading to fatigue and listlessness. Thus, the bowler may not attain maximum potency during subsequent spells. A captain must know how to employ his bowling resources optimally. If he finds that the wicket is turning considerably, he should put the spinners into operation, at the earliest, and if they prove successful, he should continue with them, even if he has the best possible pacemen at his disposal. An astute captain assesses his opponents carefully and employs his bowlers and fielders to constantly exert pressure on them. He does his job with purposeful urgency on the field and does not waste time. He ensures that fielding changes are done quickly, with the maximum utilisation of time.

The captain, obviously, has the final authority on the field regarding how to use his batsmen, bowlers and fielders. Nevertheless, it would be prudent on his part to discuss matters with other senior and experienced cricketers, who would definitely provide some helpful contributions. Further, a captain should allow enough leeway for senior bowlers to set their own field but can advise them to change it if he feels it is absolutely necessary.

A captain must not hesitate to change the batting order, whenever the situation so demands. If his decision pays off, the players will gain more confidence in the captain's astute knowledge and dexterity. A captain should prepare the batting order and inform his batsmen in advance. However, at the same time, he should caution them to be ready for changes if circumstances demand them. The players should be ready to accept the captain's decision in the overall interest of the team. The captain should ensure that all batsmen play according to his instructions to the extent possible. If a player does not follow the captain's instructions deliberately, he should be properly disciplined. The captain may decide to drop him from the team, if necessary. On the other hand, if a player fails somehow while following his captain's instructions, the latter should take full responsibility to make sure that the future of the player concerned is not adversely affected.

Both the captain and the players should always remember that the 'game is always greater than the player'. Players come and players go but cricket is there to stay. Also, no single cricketer is indispensable.

After a match is over, both rival captains should ensure that the teams get together in an informal atmosphere and enjoy themselves, cracking jokes and exchanging notes! Whatever happens on the field should be forgotten once the game is over. A lot of incidents occur on the field, some of them unpleasant and bitter. The latter type of incidents results when players lose their cool due to intense pressure, or due to an unacceptable decision by an umpire or because of ego problems. All such bitterness and misunderstandings should be left behind on the field and should not be allowed to keep on rankling.

On the field, it is considered gamesmanship to upset a batsman's concentration in order to get him out. A captain must study and assess the temperament of each batsman of the rival team and accordingly plan his strategy. The captain must know the strengths and weaknesses of his own teammates. He must not deploy an attacking field when he does not have the required pace bowlers to deliver the goods. If he does so, he could end up conceding easy runs to the batting team.

If the captain happens to be an accomplished batsman, he can extract the best from the other batsmen of his team through proper guidance and motivation. He can thus help his team build up a large total.

A captain would be well advised to include a few left-handed batsmen in the team since their style of playing could upset the line and rhythm of the rival team's bowlers because a good delivery to a right-handed batsman could prove ineffective in the case of a left-handed batsman.

The captain must instruct his batsmen to go in for quick singles, i.e., by running fast between the wickets at every opportunity. Such a move tends to upset the bowlers' rhythm and line and also the fielders' concentration. He must study the temperament of each and every player of the opposing team and set the field accordingly.

If someone misfields or drops a catch, the captain should not lose his cool because anger will not help. No cricketer likes to drop a catch or misfield deliberately. However, if someone is lethargic or slow then the captain shouldn't hesitate to pull him up and give him a piece of his mind.

Some players use negative tactics to upset the rival team's batsmen. In this regard, I recall a couple of instances; in the first case I was directly involved.

We were playing against Australia at Sydney in 1986. I had just played a stroke on the leg side, and there was a loud appeal for a catch behind the wicket. The umpire turned down the appeal but the Australians were not happy with this decision. The Australian captain started using abusive language, despite being repeatedly told that the umpire was the best judge. However, he continued with his tirade, obviously to throw the batsman off balance. Despite such irritants, I was determined not to get upset or lose my concentration. I wound up scoring 137 runs in that innings.

The second incident occurred during a test match against Australia at Madras in the 1986-87 series. We were in a winning position; we needed just a few runs to achieve victory, with a few wickets in hand. The Australians again decided to implement their gameplan of using foul language, which upset the young players. The test ultimately ended in a tie, as our batsmen ended up playing rash strokes. The point that I am emphasising here is that one should ignore such diversions, and instead concentrate on one's game, whatever be the provocation.

The captain should make sure that unsavoury and inimical incidents do not occur on the field. He can play a crucial role in maintaining discipline and control at all times.

Once a match is over, I think it becomes a duty of the home team to invite the rival team for a get-together or party in order to maintain cordial relations among the players.

After each match the captain must analyse and assess the performance of his teammates, including his own. He should be able to identify his team's weak points and try to get rid of them. Simultaneously, he should point out the strong points and develop them even further. A captain should learn lessons from every match.

Apart from his role on the field, the captain has to maintain good public relations, off the field, with the media. After a match, the captain should thank the organisers, either verbally or in written form. A simple word of thanks or a thank-you note makes a positive impact. He should be able to speak cogently and articulate his thoughts clearly and succinctly. A captain should be a *leader* in the true sense of the term.

Nine
Fighting Fit

Physical fitness plays an important role in any cricketer's success. I have always believed that in the present-day cricketing world there are no short cuts to success except hard work and constant physical fitness. If one is talented and physically fit, then the sky is the limit for such a player. I have noticed that today's players are much fitter and more energetic than players two decades ago. Physical training for players is a must today as the game has become highly competitive. In fact, many talented players could not make it to top-level cricket mainly due to lack of physical fitness.

Let me recount my own experiences in this context. I could make many comebacks because of persistent and determined hard work and by achieving the physical fitness level demanded by international cricket. I could amass those large scores and could concentrate much more intensely because of my physical fitness.

Once, when I was dropped from the Indian team, I realised that only physical fitness could help me regain my place. I strongly contend that the off-season period is the best time to concentrate on achieving physical fitness. While caught up in the flurry of hectic activity during a series, one cannot really devote much time to regular and systematic exercise.

Physical fitness is an essential element of any successful cricketer's overall characteristics. Such fitness leads to a positive frame of mind. For instance, the legendary Australian paceman Denis Lillee could make a comeback (after suffering a serious back injury) because of intense and disciplined physical exercises, which ensured his fitness. Similarly, in 1983, Imran Khan was seriously injured on his shin, which could have finished his career. But sheer determination and regular training helped Imran in overcoming all obstacles in his way. He was also instrumental in boosting Pakistan's prospects in world cricket.

Initially, Sunil Gavaskar was not a great 'fan' of physical fitness. But once he crossed the age of 30, and started playing an increasing number of one-day fixtures, he too realised the significance of physical fitness for survival in the fiercely competitive international arena. He began concentrating seriously on this aspect after that.

A player's state of physical fitness can be easily ascertained. If he is in a bad shape for example, after taking two or three runs, he would hardly be in a condition to face and play the next delivery, and he would be huffing and puffing to get his breath back. Any intelligent and experienced bowler will not hesitate to have a go at an exhausted batsman before he can recover.

Moreover, a bowler does not get a chance to bowl at peak form unless he chases a few shots racing to the boundary. Also the wicket-keeper, if not physically fit, could drop catches and fumble with the ball due to lack of concentration, which is a consequence of lack of physical fitness, especially if he has batted earlier for a long spell. I feel that lack of concentration can be attributed to lack of physical fitness.

People normally raise the query: what exactly is 'fitness'? In my opinion fitness can be defined as follows: It is the ability to withstand maximum stress, the ability to play at peak form for six hours or more, without feeling tired. This applies basically to batsmen and fielders (including the wicket-keeper). As regards bowlers, fitness would mean the capacity to bowl a long initial spell, without becoming tired, and then coming back for the subsequent spells and bowling with the same fire and hostility (for a pace bowler), and with the same line, length and accuracy (for a spinner).

All Indian players subscribe to total physical fitness at present. For instance, Kapil Dev started training at a very young age and he firmly believes that it is complete physical fitness that has contributed to his overall success in all aspects of the game — bowling, batting and fielding. He contends that physical fitness achieved during off-season periods helped him in bowling long spells over and over again without fatigue or lapse of concentration. Kapil began his test career in 1978 and only recently announced his plan to retire. A truly remarkable accomplishment! Even as a boy, he would go in for energetic jogging, sprinting and stretching exercises. Also, he would bowl at the nets for as long as possible till the point of exhaustion.

DIFFERENT METHODS FOR KEEPING FIT
There are various methods for keeping fit. If one can combine all these methods, such a combination would prove ideal in achieving and maintaining complete physical fitness. Let us now discuss these exercises individually.

Jogging
Jogging is a must and one should jog as much as possible, especially in the off-season period. About 20 minutes of jogging is essential, preferably on a grass surface in order to gain some support. It is important to do at least eight rounds of a cricket field (if one jogs leisurely, one can complete one round in about 2.5 minutes). I do not recommend running on paved roads because of potential risk of injury to the ankles, calves, shin, knees or back because of the surface being hard. One should undertake jogging on paved roads only if one has the appropriate shoes with adequate padding and cushioning which can absorb the impact of the foot on the road effectively.

Skipping

Skipping also is a must for cricketers, specially for batsmen, in order to improve their foot work. I started skipping at a very young age and would do anything between 2000 and 3000 skips daily. This not only helps to strengthen one's legs but also makes an arch under the feet which helps one to move the feet quickly both against pace and spin. I think most of the leading Indian cricketers do a lot of skipping for improving their foot work. Try to do single skips and make sure the rope comes over your head and doesn't stop at any point. Try to do more without a break so that you could build up good stamina also. Skipping is a good exercise to keep yourself fit even for general fitness.

Cycling

This is another sport that helps you to strengthen your legs and gives good exercise to your heart and lungs. Try to start with half an hour cycling and then increase the duration. Adjust your seat to such a height that when you pedal your bicycle, at the lowest point, your leg stays straight so that there would be less strain on your knees.

The foregoing discussion is to remind you to try to go in for as much physical training as possible but more in the off-season. Try to work out in a group so that it could be fun and of course you can achieve more. You need discipline for training. I know it is not an interesting activity when you are not fond of it, but one must develop a habit to do it alone which is a sign of a disciplined cricketer.

Before you start any exercise you must consult your doctor to ensure that you are not suffering from any disease. Initially, warm up your body so that you can stretch your muscles easily and properly. There are various kinds of activities. One can warm up the body through jogging, spot jogging, skipping, cycling, etc. Whether you are a batsman, bowler, fielder, or wicket-keeper, you need stamina, speed, mobility, and quick reflexes. These qualities can be acquired only if you work hard for your fitness. It is very important to stretch and strengthen your muscles so that you don't face any problem during the game and can play for long periods without any sign of tiredness.

Training is important for both senior and junior players. And it is always useful to maintain discipline. West Indian cricketers were virtually unbeatable between 1976 and 1985, because they were a very fit, sincere, and ambitious lot. They were also lucky to find a physio like Dennis Wright who looked after injuries and worked hard to ensure the team's fitness. Seniors and juniors worked together and those who couldn't take the hectic schedules and workouts and showed lack of discipline couldn't survive for long.

I have always been a great believer in fitness and could play for nearly two decades because of regular training. I don't remember having any muscle injury during play. I used to do my own set of exercises which I picked up from books, by watching people doing it, and trying them at home and later on including them in my repertoire. I must confess that they have been very effective and helped me to play for such long periods. You must stretch your muscles before any kind of game and avoid injuries, specially in cold weather, when one tends to suffer more due to injuries.

I always perform my exercise first in a standing position and then on the ground. Always start your exercises from your feet and finish with neck exercises. I will start with exercises for the ankles.

Ankles

When you are running there is always great strain on your ankles. To reduce this strain you could try the following method: You should stand on one leg; lift your other leg and rotate your foot and circle it to your right, then to left, up and down, at least ten times. Next, change your legs and do the same with the other foot.

Calf Muscles

Pace bowlers sometimes do have problems with their calf muscles because of insufficient stretching. Any small stiffness in any muscle restricts the mechanism of the body. To counteract this, place your hands on a wall and take your feet back so that they are in a position where your heels stay a couple of inches above the ground. Try to touch the ground with one heel and then with the other one. Next, keep both heels together on the ground for 30 seconds. This exercise will stretch your calf muscles very well.

Knees and Groin

The following exercise helps in stretching your knees and groin: Spread your legs with both big toes facing in the same direction. Bend your back knee, keeping it just a few inches above the ground. As you do this, your front knee will also bend. Keep your back and hands straight in front or above your head and count up to 50. Change your position and do the same with the other leg.

Hamstring A

This exercise helps in stretching your hamstring. Spread both legs to attain a comfortable position, keeping your knees straight; slide down your hands and catch hold of the ankles and remain in that position for 30-45 seconds keeping your head down.

Hamstring B

This exercise also helps in stretching your hamstring. Spread your legs to a comfortable position. Keeping your knees straight, go down to one side with both hands together. Rock your body 10 times (going down and coming up). Change your position and repeat the exercise with the other side.

Hamstring C

Again, spread both your legs, keeping the knees straight. Go down, touching the left foot with the right hand and the right foot with the left hand. Now, perform this exercise rhythmically without stopping. Do it at least 20 times to start with and then increase to 50 times.

This exercise is ideal for stretching your hamstring or side muscles of your trunk and ribs, which a cricketer uses a lot during batting and bowling.

Hamstring D

Stand straight, keeping both legs together. Go down slowly, keeping knees straight; try to touch the ground; come back and repeat the exercise at least 20 times. Or else, just go down, with the hands resting on the ground, stay there for 30 seconds, keeping your back straight. This exercise will stretch your hamstring and calf muscles.

Hamstring E

Cross your legs; go down slowly and stay in that position for 30 seconds. Interchange the legs and do the same with the other leg or go down and touch the ground and come up; repeat 10 times. If you have problems with your back, go down up to 45 degrees looking straight and stay there for some time or rock up and down. After this exercise you would feel your hamstring stretching. Lift one leg high. Clasp with both hands under your leg. Repeat ten times with each leg.

Knees

All muscles and joints are important but the knees play a crucial role in moving about. Knee problems make it difficult to run around, so it's important to stretch the knees properly. Stand straight with the legs slightly spread out. Bend both knees, try to touch the back of your heels with hands, keeping the body weight on the balls of your feet. Repeat the procedure 10-20 times.

Stretching of Waist and Ribs

This is the easiest and the most relaxing exercise. Stand straight, with the legs slightly apart. Swing both your arms, first to the left and then to the right keeping them up to chest height. Repeat about 20 times.

One must stretch the side muscles so that one can move freely. This exercise is useful especially for bowlers because they have to do a lot of turning and twisting. Spread your legs to a comfortable position, keeping one hand near the ear and bending to the other side (keeping the hand on the side of the leg and sliding it down). Repeat at least 20 times on each side.

Shoulder and Neck

A player has to loosen his shoulder muscles in order to play properly. For this he should swing his arms forward 20 times and backward 20 times. Also the following exercises prove handy:

1. Lift your shoulders up to your ears and relax; repeat the process 20 times.
2. Take your hands up together keeping them straight and try to reach the ceiling and relax. Repeat 20 times. This stretches the shoulders.
3. Clasp your hands behind your head and try and pull them apart. Repeat 5 times. This exercise is good for stretching the shoulders.
4. One must stretch the neck muscles to enable free movement of the head. Stand straight, with legs apart and hands resting behind your back. Rotate the neck in a circular motion, clockwise, with the chin touching the chest at the end of the motion. Repeat 10 times. Then repeat the exercise in the anticlockwise direction.
5. Take your head back as much as possible with the eyes looking at the sky and bring the head down again with the chin touching the chest. Repeat 10 times.
6. Bend your head to the right, touching the shoulder; then bend it towards the left. Repeat 10 times.

FLOOR EXERCISES
You also need to do some floor exercises in order to be fully fit for any game. As a matter of fact, you stretch the same muscles but in different positions.

Groin
1. Sit on the floor with knees bent on either side, with the feet touching. Hold your feet and try to pull them towards your body and try to press the knees towards the ground as much as possible. Do this exercise rhythmically pressing up and down at least 10 times. This is good for stretching the groin.
2. This exercise helps in stretching your groin and muscles behind the knee joints. Spread your legs as far as possible, keeping both hands together, trying to go down as much forward as possible.
3. Keep the legs initially straight. Bend the right leg sideways. Hold the right ankle and pull away from the body. This will make an 'L' shape. Do the same with the other leg. You stretch both your quadriceps and groin with this exercise.

Back and Hamstring
Keep both legs straight and together. Hold your toes with the hands and pull them towards the body. You will feel the back and the hamstring stretching.

It is important to keep the back strong but loose to enable you to move quickly whether you are a batsman, bowler, fielder or keeper since you have to bend forward virtually the whole day, straining the back. Always stretch your back before and after the game.

MORE BACK EXERCISES

1. Lie on your back. Keep one leg straight; bend the other leg and pull it towards the chest. Hold for at least 15 seconds. Repeat 2-3 times with each leg. This will stretch the hip and back muscles.
2. Bend both knees and bring them towards the chest, lying on your back. Encircle the knees with your arms and pull them towards the chest. Hold this position for 15-20 seconds.
3. Lie on your back, with the hands stretched on both sides. Bend your knees towards the chest and then let the knees go down towards the left. Hold for 30 seconds. Repeat the procedure, bending towards the right, keeping arms stretched at all times.

One should do a set of exercises to strengthen the stomach muscles and the spine as well, which are as follows:

1. Lie on your back and bend your knees, keeping both feet on the ground. Ask someone to stand on your feet so that you can balance properly. Keeping the hands behind your head, come up towards the knees and go back, making sure that the head does not touch the ground. Repeat 25 times to start with, gradually increasing the frequency. You can make some alterations in this exercise also. Stay in the same position but slide your feet forward slightly, keeping hands along the sides of the body. Come up and go back. Repeat rhythmically 50 times. This exercise will strengthen your stomach muscles.
2. Spread your arms, lying on your back, keeping both legs together. Lift your legs up to 90 degrees; lower them without touching the ground. Lift them again without any support making the stomach muscles do the job. Repeat 20 times, increasing to 50 times gradually. This exercise strengthens the lower abdominal muscles.
3. The best exercise to get rid of spinal stiffness is to roll on your back at least 10 times.
4. Lie on your stomach, keeping both hands behind your head. Lift the upper half of the body as much as possible. If you are having problems doing this exercise, ask someone to hold your ankles. Repeat 20 times.

WEIGHT TRAINING AND DIET

Weight training is also important. Many players refrained from such training in the past, but I feel that such training not only strengthens your muscles but also gives you more power and energy. Cricket is now a game of power and speed. Make sure you use weights properly, keeping in mind the kind of game you are playing and which muscles need strengthening. It's usually better to have someone around who has the experience to direct you regarding the weights to use and the methods of using them.

Always start with light weights and increase gradually. I feel that weight training is essential, provided it is done properly and professionally.

Diet plays an important part in any sportsman's life. Hard work but poor diet is not good for the body. This will leave you feeling weak and can affect your performance. It is not necessary to be a non-vegetarian to become a cricketer; vegetarian food is as good as non-veg. As a matter of fact, there is more choice in vegetarian foods. There are different kinds of pulses, chick-peas, etc., which are rich in protein and which can replace meat and chicken. As a vegetarian, you can bowl fast, become a good batsman, wicket-keeper and fielder. Always include milk, fruit and green vegetables in the diet, not forgetting the humble potato. Foods rich in carbohydrates like rice and pasta increase energy. Work hard and eat well to retain energy.

CONCLUSION

After going through this chapter, I hope you realise that fitness plays an important part in a cricketer's success. Do not forget to do your exercises at least six times a week, with a day off for rest. The body is like a machine; if used properly it will give you good service. Irregular use makes it rusty. Look after your body. There is nothing better than a healthy body. Always make time for your daily exercise routine, despite a busy schedule. People tend to fork out various excuses for not doing exercises. Nevertheless, I seriously suggest you make it a daily habit either outdoors or indoors. I tend to do my jogging and exercises on the beach which I find very refreshing.

Mohinder Amarnath performing stretching exercises to keep in trim

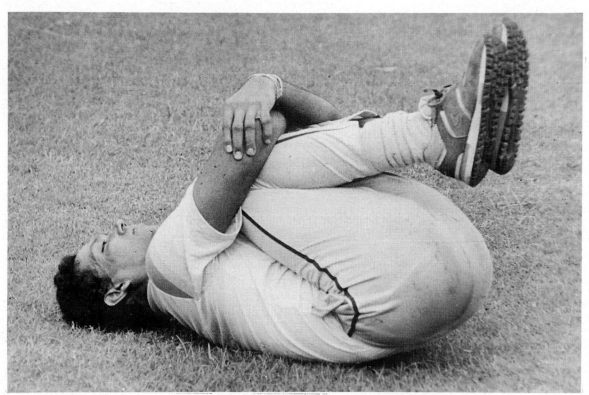

The author remaining 'fighting fit' through regular exercise

The author in 'driving' action

Mohinder Amarnath executing the hook

The author following the ball's
trajectory after a leg side shot

Mohinder Amarnath demonstrates the sweep

Ten
The Role of the Manager/Coach

The manager's job is as important as that of the captain of the team. Of course, the captain is the leader of the team, but the manager also helps in planning the strategy and tactics which should be chalked out properly. The manager should be as involved with the game as the players, although he shall not be stepping on to the field during the game but he can always lift the morale of the team with pep talk before and during the game.

In my long cricketing career, I have toured with many former cricket-playing managers. They were all renowned players in their days but some of them were just not fit enough for the job; either they were too old or just couldn't communicate with the players. There often was a communication gap between the players and the manager, and the team suffered because of the lack of rapport.

I have seen managers come in their elegant suits, nicely dressed. They would go to the ground, take off their jacket, look at the wicket, gossip, joke around with friends, have lunch with VIPs or board officials and would feel that they had done their job wonderfully well.

Now the times have changed and I would hate to have such a manager because I always felt that the manager should be a part of the team and should be fit enough to practise with the players. We require a relatively young manager who has retired a few years back and is aware of the current and modern tactics of the game. According to me the ideal manager should have the following qualities:

1. He should be an ex-player with a good deal of experience and several achievements to his credit so that no one can question his credentials.
2. He should be relatively young and fit enough to spend more time with the players, and participate keenly in practice sessions.
3. If a player is facing problems in any department of the game, he should have the ability to pinpoint the mistake and be able to rectify it.
4. The players must have faith in his abilities and should have a good rapport with

him to enable them to discuss any issue pertaining to cricket at any time of the day.

5. He should be well respected and impartial.

THE DUTIES OF A MANAGER

1. He must make sure that all the players are well informed about the laws and rules of the game or tournament.
2. He must ensure the fitness of each player before and during the game.
3. He must know details of the strengths and weaknesses of the opposition and plan accordingly. With high-tech gadgets available today he should get video tapes of his team and the opposing team to plan his strategy.
4. He should watch and analyse carefully the game and make notes and discuss the details with the players later on.
5. Prior to the net practice, he must check the wicket, nets, run-up and even the ground where the players are due to practise to make sure that nets are of good quality and there are no gaps in them. He should ensure that the playing wicket is properly rolled, the run-up is smooth and there are no holes in the outfield because any injury to a player can cause problems.
6. He must check that the footwear to be worn by the players, both spikes and rubbers, are in good condition, and also that players are well dressed and their gear is in top condition.
7. He should ensure discipline both on and off the field but should not be too autocratic.
8. He must spend time with players both on and off the field to ease out any tension and rectify mistakes.
9. He must take care of the players' welfare and give equal personal attention to all of them.
10. He should be able to motivate and encourage the team members to give off their best and boost their morale when their spirits are low.
11. In spite of maintaining team discipline, the players should be able to approach him at all times with any problem that they might have.
12. He should make sure that there is harmony between his team and the opposing team to enable the players to maintain the lofty traditions and principles of the game.
13. He should be a good diplomat.
14. For players he should be not only their friend, philosopher and guide, but also a tactician, psychologist and nurse.
15. He should possess a good sense of humour.
16. He should be able to communicate effectively, especially with the media.

Eleven
Kit Fit

Cricket is called a 'gentleman's game'. It is a game which represents honourable sportsmanship. It also demands a great deal of attention to one's equipment. It's important to have a good appearance on the field. You need not buy expensive gear, just make sure its quality is good. I have seen teams coming on to the field in shabby gear which does not create a good impression. Clothes should be neat and clean, and the boots properly polished or spruced up. It's important for a coach to check that the players are attired properly.

Buy good and durable equipment. Take a professional's advice before going out to buy the gear.

BATS

The bats have changed a lot over the years. Earlier, players wielded light bats, which was one reason why they could play a lot of strokes. Heavy bats are in vogue these days. Consequently, one hits the ball much harder and even a mishit may occasionally clear the ground.

Most of the top stars like Clive Lloyd, Viv Richards, Ian Botham, Kapil Dev and Imran Khan liked to play with heavy bats and were able to do so because they had the strength and build. A lot of youngsters try and use heavy bats to emulate their heroes, but land up in trouble as they find it difficult to even lift the bats. Heavy bats are effective on hard wickets where you play straight and more off the front foot. The ideal weight of a bat for a stroke player is 2.4 to 2.6 lbs to enable him to play his strokes freely and easily. Select a bat that you find easy to lift. Light bats are good for stroke players as they are easier to lift and have a good swing. Hence, you can play your strokes fluently and smoothly.

Presently, you get bats with polycoating and hence do not need oiling. Otherwise, bats need oiling regularly to prevent the wood from going dry. For oiling, first of all scrape the bat with fine sand paper and then apply a few drops of linseed oil to keep it in good condition.

The bat means 'bread and butter' to a batsman; so he should look after it carefully. The rubber grip of the bat is important and when you feel that it is getting worn out and that your hand is slipping, replace the grip. A lot of people prefer to use an extra grip as they find it more comfortable. Whether using one or two grips, the basic idea is to be able to grip the handle properly. I used to like the grip to be a bit thin at the top and a bit thick at the middle and bottom. You can use some tape under the grip to thicken it. Remember that an extra grip means adding extra weight to the bat.

The best way to select a good quality bat is to bounce a good quality leather ball in the middle of the bat. A high bounce shows the quality of the bat.

Wood with broad grains indicates hard wood; such wood takes time to get seasoned but once seasoned it lasts for a long time. The best way to season the bat is to give high catches or fielding practice by hitting the ball repeatedly in the middle of the bat.

Bats with narrow grains are, no doubt, good bats, but they don't last for a long time, but as long as you use them they give good service. A bat must have 8-10 (or more) grains in the blade.

The trousers and the shirt should be comfortable and loose so that you can run comfortably and bowl without any restrictions.

Any bowler's success depends on his shoes: a bowler cannot achieve much without a good pair of shoes. Most bowlers bowl with spiked shoes, with the spikes in good condition in order to provide a firm grip at the time of delivering the ball. When procuring shoes for yourself, please ensure that there is sufficient padding in the heels so that you do not get jarred. You should preferably bowl with leather sole spike shoes, as they will be handy on hard wickets. Also, wear a pair of thick socks to ensure more cushioning.

If you are essentially a batsman, wear a proper pair of shoes so that you don't have problems running between the wickets. One must check to see that no spikes are missing if you are planning to bat with spiked shoes. Shoes should be in good condition because worn-out shoes may slip on the ground. If the wicket is green and damp it's better to bat with full spikes or half spikes. I remember playing a match in Australia against the New Zealanders at Perth in 1986 on a green top wicket. K. Srikkant went into bat with rubber shoes. He played a stroke and went for a run but slipped because he was wearing the wrong pair of shoes. He must have got up and slipped and fallen at least six times trying desperately to reach the non-striker's end and was finally run out, yards out of the crease. So, remember to wear proper shoes during batting.

PROTECTIVE GEAR

It is very important to wear proper protective gear. Every cricketer must wear an athletic support or one with a pocket that will contain a box. All batsmen, close-in fielders and wicket-keepers must wear a protective box. The thigh pad is a must for a batsman so that he does not bruise his thigh while playing against any kind of bowler. If you are a right-handed batsman this pad should be worn on the left thigh and if you are a left-handed batsman this pad should be worn on the right thigh.

Batting gloves should be comfortable and should provide good protection because you get hit quite a lot against the quickies and good padding is also very important. One must be able to feel the handle of the bat so that one can hold it comfortably while wearing gloves. Preferably, one should use leather gloves.

Pads should be light and comfortable and must have good padding, so that you do not feel the impact directly if the ball hits the pad. Ensure more padding in the front pad and around the knee area. Make sure that once you buckle the pads properly, the straps don't hang out. If they are still dangling then cut them short, otherwise you may trip over them.

It has always been a good idea to bat with a cap on so that you can avoid the glare of the sun and you can concentrate more on the bowler's hand. Nowadays, of course, helmets are needed against fast and medium pace bowlers.

Some players complain of a stiff back after batting for long hours or after long spells of bowling. It's always better to change your shirt after each session so that the body stays dry especially the upper part and the back. Do not keep wearing a shirt dripping with sweat. A fresh shirt for each session will help you to avoid a stiff back.

In cold weather change your sweaty shirt immediately and put on a woollen sweater to keep your body warm. Even a vest inside the shirt helps you stay warm.

Always remember to look after your gear carefully and store it in a clean and safe condition during the off season so that when you use it again it is ready to serve you better.

Appendix
The Laws of Cricket*

LAW 1 : THE PLAYERS

1. Number of Players and Captain
A match is played between two sides each of eleven Players, one of whom shall be Captain. In the event of the Captain not being available at any time a Deputy shall act for him.

2. Nomination of Players
Before the toss for innings, the Captain shall nominate his Players who may not thereafter be changed without the consent of the opposing Captain.

Notes
(a) More or Less than Eleven Players a Side:
   A match may be played by agreement between sides of more or less than eleven players but not more than eleven players may field.

LAW 2 : SUBSTITUTES AND RUNNERS;
BATSMAN OR FIELDSMAN LEAVING THE FIELD;
BATSMAN RETIRING;
BATSMAN COMMENCING INNINGS

1. Substitutes
In normal circumstances, a Substitute shall be allowed to field only for a player who satisfies the Umpires that he has become injured or become ill during the match. However, in very exceptional circumstances, the Umpires may use their discretion to

---

* Printed by kind permission of the Marylebone Cricket Club (MCC). Copies of the current edition of the *Laws of Cricket* with full notes and interpretations can be obtained from MCC at Lord's Cricket Ground, London NW8 8QN.

allow a Substitute for a player who has to leave the field or does not take the field for other wholly acceptable reasons, subject to consent being given by the opposing Captain. If a player wishes to change his shirt, boots, etc., he may leave the field to do so (no changing on the field) but no Substitute will be allowed.

2. Objection to Substitutes
The opposing Captain shall have no right of objection to any player acting as Substitute in the field, nor as to where he shall field, although he may object to the Substitute acting as Wicket-Keeper.

3. Substitute Not to Bat or Bowl
A Substitute shall not be allowed to bat or bowl.

4. A Player for Whom a Substitute Has Acted
A player may bat, bowl or field even though a Substitute has acted for him.

5. Runner
A Runner shall be allowed for a Batsman who during the match is incapacitated by illness or injury. The player acting as Runner shall be a member of the batting side and shall, if possible, have already batted in that innings.

6. Runner's Equipment
The player acting as Runner for an injured Batsman shall wear the same external protective equipment as the injured Batsman.

7. Transgression of the Laws by an Injured Batsman or Runner
An injured Batsman may be out should his Runner break any one of Laws 33 (Handled the Ball), 37 (Obstructing the Field) or 38 (Run Out). As Striker he remains himself subject to the Laws. Furthermore, should he be out of his ground for any purpose and the wicket at the Wicket-Keeper's end be put down he shall be out under Law 38 (Run Out) or Law 39 (Stumped) irrespective of the position of the other Batsman or the Runner and no runs shall be scored.

When not the Striker, the injured Batsman is out of the game and shall stand where he does not interfere with the play. Should he bring himself into the game in any way then he shall suffer the penalties that any transgression of the Laws demands.

8. Fieldsman Leaving the Field
No Fieldsman shall leave the field or return during a session of play without the consent of the Umpire at the Bowler's end. The Umpire's consent is also necessary if a Substitute is required for a Fieldsman, when his side returns to the field after an interval. If a member of the fielding side leaves the field or fails to return after an interval and is

absent from the field for longer than 15 minutes, he shall not be permitted to bowl after his return until he has been on the field for at least that length of playing time for which he was absent. This restriction shall not apply at the start of a new day's play.

9. Batsman Leaving the Field or Retiring

A Batsman may leave the field or retire at any time owing to illness, injury or other unavoidable cause, having previously notified the Umpire at the Bowler's end. He may resume his innings at the fall of a wicket, which for the purposes of this Law shall include the retirement of another Batsman.

If he leaves the field or retires for any other reason he may only resume his innings with the consent of the opposing Captain.

When a Batsman has left the field or retired and is unable to return owing to illness, injury or other unavoidable cause, his innings is to be recorded as "retired, not out". Otherwise it is to be recorded as "retired, out".

10. Commencement of a Batsman's Innings

A Batsman shall be considered to have commenced his innings once he has stepped on to the field of play.

Notes

(a) Substitutes and Runners :

  For the purpose of these Laws allowable illnesses or injuries are those which occur at any time after the nomination by the Captains of their teams.

LAW 3 : THE UMPIRES

1. Appointment

Before the toss for innings two Umpires shall be appointed, one for each end, to control the game with absolute impartiality as required by the Laws.

2. Change of Umpire

No Umpire shall be changed during a match without the consent of both Captains.

3. Special Conditions

Before the toss for innings, the Umpires shall agree with both Captains on any special conditions affecting the conduct of the match.

4. The Wickets

The Umpires shall satisfy themselves before the start of the match that the wickets are properly pitched.

5. Clock or Watch

The Umpires shall agree between themselves and inform both Captains before the start of the match on the watch or clock to be followed during the match.

6. Conduct and Implements

Before and during a match the Umpires shall ensure that the conduct of the game and the implements used are strictly in accordance with the Laws.

7. Fair and Unfair Play

The Umpires shall be the sole judges of fair and unfair play.

8. Fitness of Ground, Weather and Light

(a) The Umpires shall be the sole judges of the fitness of the ground, weather and light for play.

   (i) However, before deciding to suspend play or not to start play or not to resume play after an interval or stoppage, the Umpires shall establish whether both Captains (the Batsmen at the wicket may deputise for their Captain) wish to commence or to continue in the prevailing conditions; if so, their wishes shall be met.

   (ii) In addition, if during play, the Umpires decide that the light is unfit, only the batting side shall have the option of continuing play. After agreeing to continue to play in unfit light conditions, the Captain of the batting side (or a Batsman at the wicket) may appeal against the light to the Umpires, who shall uphold the appeal only if, in their opinion, the light has deteriorated since the agreement to continue was made.

(b) After any suspension of play, the Umpires, unaccompanied by any of the Players or Officials shall, on their own initiative, carry out an inspection immediately (*sic*) the conditions improve and shall continue to inspect at intervals. Immediately the Umpires decide that play is possible they shall call upon the Players to resume the game.

9. Exceptional Circumstances

In exceptional circumstances, other than those of weather, ground or light, the Umpires may decide to suspend or abandon play. Before making such decision the Umpires shall establish, if the circumstances allow, whether both Captains (the Batsmen at the wicket may deputise for their Captain) wish to continue in the prevailing conditions : if so their wishes shall be met.

10. Position of Umpires

The Umpires shall stand where they can best see any act upon which their decision may be required.

Subject to this overriding consideration the Umpire at the Bowler's end shall stand where he does not interfere with either the Bowler's run-up or the Striker's view.

The Umpire at the Striker's end may elect to stand on the off instead of the leg side of the pitch, provided he informs the Captain of the fielding side and the Striker of his intention to do so.

11. Umpires Changing Ends
The Umpires shall change ends after each side has had one innings.

12. Disputes
All disputes shall be determined by the Umpires and if they disagree the actual state of things shall continue.

13. Signals
The following code of signals shall be used by Umpires who will wait until a signal has been answered by a Scorer before allowing the game to proceed:

Boundary: by waving the arm from side to side.
Boundary 6:   by raising both arms above the head.
Bye: by raising an open hand above the head.
Dead ball: by crossing and re-crossing the wrists below the waist.
Leg bye: by touching a raised knee with the hand.
No ball: by extending one arm horizontally.
Out: by raising the index finger above the head. If not out the Umpire shall call "not out".
Short run: by bending the arm upwards and by touching the nearer shoulder with the tips of the fingers.
Wide: by extending both arms horizontally.

14. Correctness of Scores
The Umpires shall be responsible for satisfying themselves on the correctness of the scores throughout and at the conclusion of the match. See Law 21.6 (Correctness of Result).

Notes
(a) Attendance of Umpires :
   The Umpires should be present on the ground and report to the Ground Executive or the equivalent at least 30 minutes before the start of a day's play.
(b) Consultation between Umpires and Scorers :
   Consultation between Umpires and Scorers over doubtful points is essential.
(c) Fitness of Ground :
   The Umpires should consider the ground as unfit for play when it is so wet or slippery as to deprive the Bowlers of a reasonable foothold, the Fieldsmen, other than the deep

---

fielders, of the power of free movement, or the Batsmen the ability to play their strokes or to run between the wickets. Play should not be suspended merely because the grass and the ball are wet and slippery.

(d) Fitness of Weather and Light:
The Umpires should only suspend play when they consider that the conditions are so bad that it is unreasonable or dangerous to continue.

LAW 4 : THE SCORERS

1. Recording Runs
All runs scored shall be recorded by Scorers appointed for the purpose. Where there are two Scorers they shall frequently check to ensure that the score sheets agree.

2. Acknowledging Signals
The Scorers shall accept and immediately acknowledge all instructions and signals given to them by the Umpires.

LAW 5 : THE BALL

1. Weight and Size
The ball, when new, shall weigh not less than 5½ ounces/155.9 g, nor more than 5¾ ounces/163 g : and shall measure not less than 8.13/16 inches/22.4 cm nor more than 9 inches/22.9 cm in circumference.

2. Approval of Balls
All balls used in matches shall be approved by the Umpires and Captains before the start of the match.

3. New Ball
Subject to agreement to the contrary, having been made before the toss, either Captain may demand a new ball at the start of each innings.

4. New Ball in Match of Three or More Days' Duration
In a match of three or more days' duration, the Captain of the fielding side may demand a new ball after the prescribed number of overs has been bowled with the old one. The Governing Body for cricket in the country concerned shall decide the number of overs applicable in that country which shall be not less than 75 six-ball overs (55 eight-ball overs).

5. Ball Lost or Becoming Unfit for Play
In the event of a ball during play being lost or, in the opinion of the Umpires, becoming

unfit for play, the Umpires shall allow it to be replaced by one that in their opinion has had a similar amount of wear. If a ball is to be replaced, the Umpires shall inform the Batsmen.

Notes

(a) Specifications :

The specifications, as described above, shall apply to top-grade balls only. The following degrees of tolerance will be acceptable for other grades of ball:

(i) *Men's Grades 2-4 :*
Weight : 5.5/16 ounces/150 g to 5.13/16 ounces/165 g
Size : 8.11/16 inches/22.0 cm to 9.1/16 inches/23.0 cm

(ii) *Women's :*
Weight : 4.15/16 ounces/140 g to 5.5/16 ounces/150g
Size : 8.1/4 inches/21.0 cm to 8.7/8 inches/22.5 cm

(iii) *Junior*
Weight : 4.5/16 ounces/133 g to 5.11/16 ounces/143 g
Size : 8.1/16 inches/20.5 cm to 8.11/16 inches/22.0 cm

LAW 6 : THE BAT

1. Width and Length

The bat overall shall not be more than 38 inches/96.5 cm in length; the blade of the bat shall be made of wood and shall not exceed 4 ¼ inches/10.8 cm at the widest part.

Notes

(a) *The blade of the bat may be covered with material for protection, strengthening or repair, Such material shall not exceed 1/16 inches/1.56 mm in thickness.*

LAW 7 : THE PITCH

1. Area of Pitch

The pitch is the area between the bowling creases — See Law 9 (The Bowling, Popping and Return Creases). It shall measure 5 ft./1.52 m in width on either side of a line joining the centre of the middle stumps of the wickets — See Law 8 (The Wickets).

2. Selection and Preparation

Before the toss for innings, the Executive of the Ground shall be responsible for the selection and preparation of the pitch; thereafter the Umpires shall control its use and maintenance.

3. Changing Pitch
The pitch shall not be changed during a match unless it becomes unfit for play, and then only with the consent of both Captains.

4. Non-Turf Pitches
In the event of a non-turf pitch being used, the following shall apply:
(a) Length : That of the playing surface to a minimum of 58 ft (17.68 m).
(b) Width : That of the playing surface to a minimum of 6 ft (1.83 m).
See Law 10 (Rolling, Sweeping, Mowing, Watering the Pitch and Re-marking of Creases) Note (a).

LAW 8 : THE WICKETS

1. Width and Pitching
Two sets of wickets, each 9 in/22.86 cm wide, and consisting of the three wooden stumps with two wooden bails upon the top, shall be pitched opposite and parallel to each other at a distance of 22 yards/20.12 m between the centres of the two middle stumps.

2. Size of Stumps
The stumps shall be of equal and sufficient size to prevent the ball from passing between them. Their tops shall be 28 in/71.1 cm above the ground, and shall be dome-shaped except for the bail grooves.

3. Size of Bails
The bails shall be each $4^3/_8$ inches/11.1 cm in length and when in position on the top of the stumps shall not project more than ½ in/1.3 cm above them.

Notes
(a) Dispensing with Bails :
  In a high wind the Umpires may decide to dispense with the use of bails.
(b) Junior Cricket :
  For Junior Cricket, as defined by the local Governing Body, the following measurements for the Wickets shall apply:-
  Width   : 8 in/20.32 cm.
  Pitch   : 21 yards/19.20 m.
  Height   : 27 in/68.58 cm.
  Bails   : each $3^7/_8$ in/9.84 cm in length and should not project more than
  *   ½ in/1.3 cm above them.*

LAW 9 : THE BOWLING, POPPING AND RETURN CREASES

1. The Bowling Crease
The bowling crease shall be marked in line with the stumps at each end and shall be 8 ft 8 in/2.64 m in length, with the stumps in the centre.

2. The Popping Crease
The popping crease, which is the back edge of the crease marking, shall be in front of and parallel with the bowling crease. It shall have the back edge of the crease marking 4 ft/1.22 m from the centre of the stumps and shall extend to a minimum of 6 ft/1.83 m on either side of the line of the wicket.

The popping crease shall be considered to be unlimited in length.

3. The Return Crease
The return crease marking, of which the inside edge is the crease, shall be at each end of the bowling crease and at right angles to it. The return crease shall be marked to a minimum of 4 ft/1.22 m behind the wicket and shall be considered to be unlimited in length. A forward extension shall be marked to the popping crease.

LAW 10 : ROLLING, SWEEPING, MOWING, WATERING THE PITCH AND RE-MARKING OF CREASES

1. Rolling
During the match the pitch may be rolled at the request of the Captain of the batting side, for a period of not more than 7 minutes before the start of each innings, other than the first innings of the match, and before the start of each day's play. In addition, if, after the toss and before the first innings of the match, the start is delayed, the Captain of the batting side shall have the right to have the pitch rolled for not more than 7 minutes.

The pitch shall not otherwise be rolled during the match.

The 7 minutes' rolling permitted before the start of a day's play shall take place not earlier than half an hour before the start of play and the Captain of the batting side may delay such rolling until 10 minutes before the start of play should he so desire.

If a Captain declares an innings closed less than 15 minutes before the resumption of play, and the other Captain is thereby prevented from exercising his option of 7 minutes rolling or if he is so prevented for any other reason the time for rolling shall be taken out of the normal playing time.

2. Sweeping
Such sweeping of the pitch as is necessary during the match shall be done so that the 7 minutes allowed for rolling the pitch provided for in (1) above is not affected.

3. Mowing

(a) *Responsibilities of Ground Authority and of Umpires :*

All mowings which are carried out before the toss for innings shall be the responsibility of the Ground Authority. Thereafter they shall be carried out under the supervision of the Umpires, see Law 7.2. (Selection and Preparation).

(b) *Initial Mowing :*

The pitch shall be mown before play begins on the day the match is scheduled to start or in the case of a delayed start on the day the match is expected to start. See 3 (a) above (Responsibilities of Ground Authority and of Umpires).

(c) *Subsequent Mowings in a Match of 2 or More Days' Duration:*

In a match of two or more days' duration, the pitch shall be mown daily before play begins. Should this mowing not take place because of weather conditions, rest days or other reasons the pitch shall be mown on the first day on which the match is resumed.

(d) *Mowing of the Outfield in a Match of 2 or More Days' Duration:*

In order to ensure that conditions are as similar as possible for both sides, the outfield shall normally be mown before the commencement of play on each day of the match, if ground and weather conditions allow. See Note (b) to this Law.

4. Watering

The pitch shall not be watered during a match.

5. Re-marking Creases

Whenever possible the creases shall be re-marked.

6. Maintenance of Foot Holes

In wet weather, the Umpires shall ensure that the holes made by the Bowlers and Batsmen are cleaned out and dried whenever necessary to facilitate play. In matches of 2 or more days' duration, the Umpires shall allow, if necessary, the returfing of foot holes made by the Bowler in his delivery stride, or the use of quick-setting fillings for the same purpose, before the start of each day's play.

7. Securing of Footholds and Maintenance of Pitch

During play, the Umpires shall allow either Batsman to beat the pitch with his bat and players to secure their footholds by the use of sawdust, provided that no damage to the pitch is so caused, and Law 42 (Unfair Play) is not contravened.

Notes

(a) Non-Turf Pitches:

Law 10 applies to turf pitches.

The game is played on non-turf pitches in many countries at various levels. Whilst the conduct of the game on these surfaces should always be in accordance with the Laws of Cricket, it is recognised that it may sometimes be necessary for Governing Bodies to lay down special playing conditions to suit the type of non-turf pitch used in their country. In matches played against Touring Teams, any special playing conditions should be agreed in advance by both parties.

(b) Mowing of the Outfield in a Match of 2 or More Days' Duration :
If, for reasons other than ground and weather conditions, daily and complete mowing is not possible, the Ground Authority shall notify the Captains and Umpires, before the toss for innings, of the procedure to be adopted for such mowing during the match.

(c) Choice of Roller :
If there is more than one roller available the Captain of the batting side shall have a choice.

LAW 11 : COVERING THE PITCH

1. Before the Start of a Match
Before the start of a match complete covering of the pitch shall be allowed.

2. During a Match
The pitch shall not be completely covered during a match unless prior arrangement or regulations so provide.

3. Covering Bowlers' Run-Up
Whenever possible, the Bowlers' run-up shall be covered, but the covers so used shall not extend further than 4 ft/1.22m, in front of the popping crease.

Notes
(a) Removal of covers
The covers should be removed as promptly as possible whenever the weather permits.

LAW 12 : INNINGS

1. Number of Innings
A match shall be of one or two innings of each side according to agreement reached before the start of play.

2. Alternate Innings
In a two-innings match each side shall take their (*sic*) innings alternately except in the case provided for in Law 13 (The Follow-On).

3. The Toss
The Captains shall toss for the choice of innings on the field of play not later than

15 minutes before the time scheduled for the match to start, or before the time agreed upon for play to start.

4. Choice of Innings   .

The winner of the toss shall notify his decision to bat or to field to the opposing Captain not later than 10 minutes before the time scheduled for the match to start, or before the time agreed upon for play to start. The decision shall not thereafter be altered.

5. Continuation after One Innings of Each Side

Despite the terms of (1) above, in a one-innings match, when a result has been reached on the first innings the Captains may agree to the continuation of play if, in their opinion, there is a prospect of carrying the game to a further issue in the time left. See Law 21 (Result).

Notes
(a) Limited Innings — One-Innings Match:
   In a one-innings match, each innings may, by agreement, be limited by a number of overs or by a period of time.
(b) Limited Innings — Two-Innings Match:
   In a two-innings match, the first innings of each side may, by agreement, be limited to a number of overs or by a period of time.

LAW 13 : THE FOLLOW-ON

1. Lead on First Innings

In a two-innings match the side which bats first and leads by 200 runs in a match of five days or more, by 150 runs in a three-day or four-day match, by 100 runs in a two-day match, or by 75 runs in a one-day match, shall have the option of requiring the other side to follow their innings.

2. Day's Play Lost

If no play takes place on the first day of a match of 2 or more days' duration, (1) above shall apply in accordance with the number of days' play remaining from the actual start of the match.

LAW 14 : DECLARATIONS

1. Time of Declaration

The Captain of the batting side may declare an innings closed at any time during a match irrespective of its duration.

2. Forfeiture of Second Innings

A Captain may forfeit his second innings, provided his decision to do so is notified to the opposing Captain and Umpires in sufficient time to allow 7 minutes rolling of the pitch. See Law 10 (Rolling, Sweeping, Mowing, Watering the Pitch and Re-marking of Creases). The normal 10-minute interval between innings shall be applied.

LAW 15 : START OF PLAY

1. Call of Play

At the start of each innings and of each day's play and on the resumption of play after any interval or interruption the Umpire at the Bowlers' end shall call "play".

2. Practice on the Field

At no time on any day of the match shall there be any bowling or batting practice on the pitch.

No practice may take place on the field if, in the opinion of the Umpires, it could result in a waste of time.

3. Trial Run-Up

No Bowler shall have a trial run-up after "play" has been called in any session of play, except at the fall of a wicket when an Umpire may allow such a trial run-up if he is satisfied that it will not cause any waste of time.

LAW 16 : INTERVALS

1. Length

The Umpire shall allow such intervals as have been agreed upon for meals, and 10 minutes between each innings.

2. Luncheon Interval — Innings Ending or Stoppage within 10 Minutes of Interval

If an innings ends or there is a stoppage caused by weather or bad light within 10 minutes of the agreed time for the luncheon interval, the interval shall be taken immediately.

The time remaining in the session of play shall be added to the agreed length of the interval but no extra allowance shall be made for the 10 minutes' interval between innings.

3. Tea Interval — Innings Ending or Stoppage within 30 Minutes of Interval

If an innings ends or there is a stoppage caused by weather or bad light within 30 minutes of the agreed time for the tea interval, the interval shall be taken immediately.

The interval shall be of the agreed length and, if applicable, shall include the 10-minute interval between innings.

4. Tea Interval — Continuation of Play

If at the agreed time for the tea interval, nine wickets are down, play shall continue for a period not exceeding 30 minutes or until the innings is concluded.

5. Tea Interval — Agreement to Forego

At any time during the match, the Captains may agree to forego a tea interval.

6. Intervals for Drinks

If both Captains agree before the start of a match that intervals for drinks may be taken, the option to take such intervals shall be available to either side. These intervals shall be restricted to one per session, shall be kept as short as possible, shall not be taken in the last hour of the match and in any case shall not exceed 5 minutes.

The agreed times for these intervals shall be strictly adhered to except that if a wicket falls within 5 minutes of the agreed time then drinks shall be taken immediately.

If an innings ends or there is a stoppage caused by weather or bad light within 30 minutes of the agreed time for a drinks interval, there will be no interval for drinks in that session.

At any time during the match the Captains may agree to forego any such drinks interval.

Notes

(a) Tea Interval — One-Day Match:

  In a one-day match, a specific time for the tea interval need not necessarily be arranged, and it may be agreed to take this interval between the innings of a one-innings match.

(b) Changing the Agreed Time of Intervals:

  In the event of the ground, weather or light conditions causing a suspension of play, the Umpires, after consultation with the Captains, may decide in the interests of time-saving, to bring forward the time of the luncheon or tea interval.

LAW 17 : CESSATION OF PLAY

1. Call of Time

The Umpire at the Bowler's end shall call "time" on the cessation of play before any interval or interruption of play, at the end of each day's play, and at the conclusion of the match. See Law 27 (Appeals)

2. Removal of Bails

After the call of "time" the Umpires shall remove the bails from both wickets.

3. Starting a Last Over

The last over before an interval or the close of play shall be started provided the

Umpire, after walking at his normal pace, has arrived at his position behind the stumps at the Bowler's end before time has been reached.

4. Completion of the Last Over of a Session
The last over before an interval or the close of play shall be completed unless a Batsman is out or retires during that over within 2 minutes of the interval or the close of play or unless the Players have occasion to leave the field.

5. Completion of the Last Over of a Match
An over in progress at the close of play on the final day of a match shall be completed at the request of either Captain even if a wicket falls after time has been reached.

If during the last over the Players have occasion to leave the field the Umpires shall call "time" and there shall be no resumption of play and the match shall be at an end.

6. Last Hour of Match — Number of Overs
The Umpires shall indicate when one hour of playing time of the match remains according to the agreed hours of play. The next over after that moment shall be the first of a minimum of 20 six-ball overs (15 eight-ball overs), provided a result is not reached earlier or there is no interval or interruption of play.

7. Last Hour of Match — Intervals between Innings and Interruptions of Play
If, at the commencement of the last hour of the match, an interval or interruption of play is in progress or if, during the last hour, there is an interval between innings or an interruption of play, the minimum number of overs to be bowled on the resumption of play shall be reduced in proportion to the duration, within the last hour of the match, of any such interval or interruption.

The minimum number of overs to be bowled after a resumption of play shall be calculated as follows:
(a) In the case of an interval or interruption of play being in progress at the commencement of the last hour of the match, or in the case of a first interval or interruption a deduction shall be made from the minimum 20 six-ball overs (or 15 eight-ball overs).
(b) If there is a later interval or interruption a further deduction shall be made from the minimum number of overs which should have been bowled following the last resumption of play.
(c) These deductions shall be based on the following factors:
   (i) the number of the overs already bowled in the last hour of the match or in the case of a later interval or interruption in the last session of play;
   (ii) the number of overs lost as a result of the interval or interruption allowing one six-ball over for every full three minutes (or one eight-ball over for every full four minutes) of interval or interruption.

> (iii) any over left uncompleted at the end of an innings to be excluded from these calculations;
>
> (iv) any over left uncompleted at the start of an interruption of play to be completed when play is resumed and to count as one over bowled; [and]
>
> (v) an interval to start with the end of an innings and to end 10 minutes later; an interruption to start on the call of 'time' and to end on the call of 'play'.

(d) In the event of an innings being completed and a new innings commencing during the last hour of the match, the number of overs to be bowled in the new innings shall be calculated on the basis of one six-ball over for every three minutes or part thereof remaining for play (or one eight-ball over for every four minutes or part thereof remaining for play); or alternatively on the basis that sufficient overs be bowled to enable the full minimum quota of overs to be completed under circumstances governed by (a), (b) and (c) above. In all such cases the alternative which allows the greater number of overs shall be employed.

8. Bowler Unable to Complete an Over during Last Hour of the Match

If, for any reason, a Bowler is unable to complete an over during the period of play referred to in (6) above, Law 22.7 (Bowler Incapacitated or Suspended during an Over) shall apply.

LAW 18 : SCORING

1. A Run

The score shall be reckoned by runs. A run is scored:

(a) So often as the Batsmen, after a hit or at any time while the ball is in play, shall have crossed and made good their ground from end to end.

(b) When a boundary is scored. See Law 19 (Boundaries).

(c) When penalty runs are awarded. See (6) below.

2. Short Runs

(a) If either Batsman runs a short run, the Umpire shall call and signal "one short" as soon as the ball becomes dead and that run shall not be scored. A run is short if a Batsman fails to make good his ground on turning for a further run.

(b) Although a short run shortens the succeeding one, the latter, if completed, shall count.

(c) If either or both Batsmen deliberately run short the Umpire shall, as soon as he sees that the fielding side has no chance of dismissing either Batsman, call and signal "dead ball" and disallow any runs attempted or previously scored. The Batsmen shall return to their original ends.

(d) If both Batsmen run short in one and the same run, only one run shall be deducted.

(e) Only if three or more runs are attempted can more than one be short and then, subject to (c) and (d) above, all runs so called shall be disallowed. If there has been more than one short run the Umpires shall instruct the Scorers as to the number of runs disallowed.

3. Striker Caught

If the Striker is caught, no run shall be scored.

4. Batsman Run Out

If a Batsman is Run Out, only that run which was being attempted shall not be scored. If, however, an injured Striker himself is run out no runs shall be scored. See Law 2.7 (Transgression of the Laws by an Injured Batsman or Runner).

5. Batsman Obstructing the Field

If a Batsman is out Obstructing the Field, any runs completed before the obstruction occurs shall be scored unless such obstruction prevents a catch being made in which case no runs shall be scored.

6. Runs Scored for Penalties

Runs shall be scored for penalties under Laws 20 (Lost Ball), 24 (No Ball), 25 (Wide Ball), 41.1 (Fielding the Ball) and for boundary allowances under Law 19 (Boundaries).

7. Batsman Returning to Wicket He Has Left

If, while the ball is in play, the Batsmen have crossed in running, neither shall return to the wicket he has left even though a short run has been called or no run has been scored as in the case of a catch. Batsmen, however, shall return to the wickets they originally left in the cases of a boundary and of any disallowance of runs and of an injured Batsman being, himself, run out. See Law 2.7 (Transgression of the Laws by an Injured Batsman or Runner).

Notes

(a) Short Run:

A Striker taking stance in front of his popping crease may run from that point without penalty.

LAW 19 : BOUNDARIES

1. The Boundary of the Playing Area

Before the toss for innings, the Umpires shall agree with both Captains on the boundary of the playing area. The boundary shall, if possible, be marked by a white line, a rope laid on the ground, or a fence. If flags or posts only are used to mark a boundary, the imaginary line joining such points shall be regarded as the boundary. An obstacle, or person, within the playing area shall not be regarded as a boundary unless so decided by the Umpires before the toss for innings. Sight screens within, or partially within, the playing area shall be regarded as the boundary and when the ball strikes or passes within or under or directly over any part of the screen, a boundary shall be scored.

2. Runs Scored for Boundaries

Before the toss for innings, the Umpires shall agree with both Captains the runs to be allowed for boundaries, and in deciding the allowance for them, the Umpires and Captains shall be guided by the prevailing custom of the ground. The allowance for a boundary shall normally be 4 runs, and 6 runs for all hits pitching over and clear of the boundary line or fence, even though the ball has been previously touched by a Fieldsman. Six runs shall also be scored if a Fieldsman, after catching a ball, carries it over the boundary. See Law 32 (Caught) Note (a). Six runs shall not be scored when a ball struck by the Striker hits a sight-screen full pitch if the screen is within, or partially within, the playing area, but if the ball is struck directly over a sight-screen so situated, 6 runs shall be scored.

3. A Boundary

A boundary shall be scored and signalled by the Umpire at the Bowler's end whenever in his opinion:
(a) A ball in play touches or crosses the boundary, however marked.
(b) A Fieldsman with ball in hand touches or grounds any part of his person on or over a boundary line.
(c) A Fieldsman with ball in hand grounds any part of his person over a boundary fence or board. This allows the Fieldsman to touch or lean on or over a boundary fence or board in preventing a boundary.

4. Runs Exceeding Boundary Allowance

The runs completed at the instant the ball reaches the boundary shall count if they exceed the boundary allowance.

5. Overthrows or Wilful Act of a Fieldsman

If the boundary results from an overthrow or from the wilful act of a Fieldsman, any runs already completed and the allowance shall be added to the score. The run in progress shall count provided that the Batsmen have crossed at the instant of the throw or act.

Notes
(a) Position of Sight-Screens:
   Sight-screens should, if possible, be positioned wholly outside the playing area, as near as possible to the boundary line.

LAW 20 : LOST BALL

1. Runs Scored
If a ball in play cannot be found or recovered any fieldsman may call "lost ball" when six runs shall be added to the score; but if more than six have been run before "lost ball" is called, as many runs as have been completed shall be scored. The run in progress shall count provided that the Batsmen have crossed at the instant of the call of "lost ball".

2. How Scored
The runs shall be added to the score of the Striker if the ball has been struck, but otherwise to the score of byes, leg-byes, no-balls or wides as the case may be.

LAW 21 : THE RESULT

1. A Win — Two-Innings Matches
The side which has scored a total of runs in excess of that scored by the opposing side in its two completed innings shall be the winners.

2. A Win — One-Innings Matches
(a) One-innings matches, unless played out as in (1) above, shall be decided on the first innings, but see Law 12.5 (Continuation after One Innings of Each Side).
(b) If the Captains agree to continue play after the completion of one innings of each side in accordance with Law 12.5 (Continuation after One Innings of Each Side) and a result is not achieved on the second innings, the first innings result shall stand.

3. Umpires Awarding a Match
(a) A match shall be lost by a side which, during the match
   (i) refuses to play, or
   (ii) concedes defeat,
and the Umpires shall award the match to the other side.
(b) Should both Batsmen at the wickets or the fielding side leave the field at any time without the agreement of the Umpires, this shall constitute a refusal to play and, on appeal, the Umpires shall award the match to the other side in accordance with (a) above.

4. A Tie
The result of a match shall be a tie when the scores are equal at the conclusion of play, but only if the side batting last has completed its innings.

    If the scores of the completed first innings of a one-day match are equal, it shall be a tie but only if the match has not been played out to a further conclusion.

5. A Draw
A match not determined in any of the ways as in 1, 2, 3 and 4 above shall count as a draw.

6. Correctness of Result
Any decision as to the correctness of the scores shall be the responsibility of the Umpires. See Law 3.14 (Correctness of Scores).

If, after the Umpires and Players have left the field, in the belief that the match has been concluded, the Umpires decide that a mistake in scoring has occurred, which affects the result, and provided time has not been reached, they shall order play to resume and to continue until the agreed finishing time unless a result is reached earlier.

If the Umpires decide that a mistake has occurred and time has been reached, the Umpires shall immediately inform both Captains of the necessary corrections to the scores and, if applicable, to the result.

7. Acceptance of Result
In accepting the scores as notified by the scorers and agreed by the Umpires, the Captains of both sides thereby accept the result.

Notes
(a) Statement of Results:

The result of a finished match is stated as win by runs, except in the case of a win by the side batting last when it is by the number of wickets still then to fall.

(b) Winning Hit or Extras:

As soon as the side has won, see 1 and 2 above, the Umpire shall call "time", the match is finished, and nothing that happens thereafter other than as a result of a mistake in scoring, see 6. above, shall be regarded as part of the match.

However, if a boundary constitutes the winning hit — or extras — and the boundary allowance exceeds the number of runs required to win the match, such runs scored shall be credited to the side's total and, in the case of a hit, to the Striker's score.

LAW 22 : THE OVER

1. Number of Balls
The ball shall be bowled from each wicket alternately in overs of either 6 or 8 balls according to agreement before the match.

2. Call of "Over"
When the agreed number of balls has been bowled, and as the ball becomes dead or when it becomes clear to the Umpire at the Bowler's end that both the fielding side and the Batsmen at the wicket have ceased to regard the ball as in play, the Umpire shall call "over" before leaving the wicket.

3. No Ball or Wide Ball
Neither a no ball nor a wide ball shall be reckoned as one of the over.

4. Umpire Miscounting
If an Umpire miscounts the number of balls, the over as counted by the Umpire shall stand.

5. Bowler Changing Ends
A Bowler shall be allowed to change ends as often as desired provided only that he does not bowl two overs consecutively in an innings.

6. The Bowler Finishing an Over
A Bowler shall finish an over in progress unless he be incapacitated or be suspended under Laws 42.8 (The Bowling of Fast Short Pitched Balls), 42.9 (The Bowling of Fast High Full Pitches), 42.10 (Time Wasting) and 42.11 (Players Damaging the Pitch). If an over is left incomplete for any reason at the start of an interval or interruption of play, it shall be finished on the resumption of play.

7. Bowler Incapacitated or Suspended during an Over
If, for any reason, a Bowler is incapacitated while running up to bowl the first ball of an over, or is incapacitated or suspended during an over, the Umpire shall call and signal "dead ball" and another Bowler shall be allowed to bowl or complete the over from the same end, provided only that he shall not bowl two overs, or part thereof, consecutively in one innings.

8. Position of Non-Striker
The Batsman at the Bowler's end shall normally stand on the opposite side of the wicket to that from which the ball is being delivered, unless a request to do otherwise is granted by the Umpire.

LAW 23 : DEAD BALL

1. The Ball Becomes Dead, When:
(a) It is finally settled in the hands of the Wicket-Keeper or the Bowler.
(b) It reaches or pitches over the boundary.
(c) A Batsman is out.
(d) Whether played or not, it lodges in the clothing or equipment of a Batsman or the clothing of an Umpire.
(e) A ball lodges in a protective helmet worn by a member of the fielding side.
(f) A penalty is awarded under Law 20 (Lost Ball) or Law 41.1 (Fielding the Ball).
(g) The Umpire calls "over" or "time".

2. Either Umpire Shall Call and Signal "Dead Ball", when:
(a) He intervenes in a case of unfair play.
(b) A serious injury to a Player or Umpire occurs.
(c) He is satisfied that, for an adequate reason, the Striker is not ready to receive the ball and makes no attempt to play it.
(d) The Bowler drops the ball accidentally before delivery, or the ball does not leave his hand for any reason.
(e) One or both bails fall from the Striker's wicket before he receives the delivery.
(f) He leaves his normal position for consultation.
(g) He is required to do so under Law 26.3 (Disallowance of Leg-Byes), etc.

3. The Ball Ceases to Be Dead, When
(a) The Bowler starts his run-up or bowling action.

4. The Ball Is Not Dead, When:
(a) It strikes an Umpire (unless it lodges in his dress).
(b) The wicket is broken or struck down (unless a Batsman is out thereby).
(c) An unsuccessful appeal is made.
(d) The wicket is broken accidentally either by the Bowler during his delivery or by a Batsman in running.
(e) The Umpire has called "no ball" or "wide".

Notes
(a) Ball Finally Settled:
Whether the ball is finally settled or not — see 1 (a) above — must be a question for the Umpires alone to decide.
(b) Action on Call of "Dead Ball":
   (i) *If "dead ball" is called prior to the Striker receiving a delivery the Bowler shall be allowed an additional ball.*
   (ii) *If "dead ball" is called after the Striker receives a delivery the Bowler shall not be allowed an additional ball, unless a "no ball" or "wide" has been called.*

LAW 24 : NO BALL

1. Mode of Delivery
The Umpire shall indicate to the Striker whether the Bowler intends to bowl over or round the wicket, overarm or underarm, or right or left-handed. Failure on the part of the Bowler to indicate in advance a change in his mode of delivery is unfair and the Umpire shall call and signal "no ball".

2. Fair Delivery — The Arm
For a delivery to be fair the ball must be bowled not thrown — see Note (a) below. If either Umpire is not entirely satisfied with the absolute fairness of a delivery in this respect he shall call and signal "no ball" instantly upon delivery.

3. Fair Delivery — The Feet
The Umpire at the bowler's wicket shall call and signal "no ball" if he is not satisfied that in the delivery stride:
(a) the Bowler's back foot has landed within and not touching the return crease or its forward extension, or
(b) some part of the front foot whether grounded or raised was behind the popping crease.

4. Bowler Throwing at Striker's Wicket before Delivery
If the Bowler, before delivering the ball, throws it at the Striker's wicket in an attempt to run him out, the Umpire shall call and signal "no ball". See Law 42.12 (Batsman Unfairly Stealing Run) and Law 38 (Run Out).

5. Bowler Attempting to Run Out Non-Striker before Delivery
If the Bowler, before delivering the ball, attempts to run out the non-Striker, any runs which result shall be allowed and shall be scored as no balls. Such an attempt shall not count as a ball in the over. The Umpire shall not call "no ball". See Law 42.12 (Batsman Unfairly Stealing a Run).

6. Infringement of Laws by a Wicket-Keeper or a Fieldsman
The Umpire shall call and signal "no ball" in the event of the Wicket-Keeper infringing Law 40.1 (Position of Wicket-Keeper) or a Fieldsman infringing Law 41.2 (Limitation of On-side Fieldsmen) or Law 41.3 (Position of Fieldsmen).

7. Revoking a Call
An Umpire shall revoke the call "no ball" if the ball does not leave the Bowler's hand for any reason. See Law 23.2 (Either Umpire Shall Call and Signal "Dead Ball").

8. Penalty
A penalty of one run for a no ball shall be scored if no runs are made otherwise.

9. Runs from a No Ball
The Striker may hit a no ball and whatever runs result shall be added to his score. Runs made otherwise from a no ball shall be scored no balls.

10. Out from a No Ball
The Striker shall be out from a no ball if he breaks Law 34 (Hit the Ball Twice) and

either Batsman may be Run Out or shall be given out if either breaks Law 33 (Handled the Ball) or Law 37 (Obstructing the Field).

11. Batsman Given Out off a No Ball

Should a Batsman be given out off a no ball the penalty for bowling it shall stand unless runs are otherwise scored.

Notes

(a) Definition of a Throw

A ball shall be deemed to have been thrown if, in the opinion of either Umpire, the process of straightening the bowling arm, whether it be partial or complete, takes place during that part of the delivery swing which directly precedes the ball leaving the hand. This definition shall not debar a bowler from the use of the wrist in the delivery swing.

(b) No Ball not Counting in Over:

A no ball shall not be reckoned as one of the over. See Law 22.3 (No Ball or Wide Ball).

LAW 25 : WIDE BALL

1. Judging a Wide

If the Bowler bowls the ball so high over or so wide off the wicket that, in the opinion of the Umpire it passes out of reach of the Striker, standing in a normal guard position, the Umpire shall call and signal "wide ball" as soon as it has passed the line of the Striker's wicket.

The Umpire shall not adjudge a ball as being a wide if:

(a) The Striker, by moving from his guard position, causes the ball to pass out of his reach.

(b) The Striker moves and thus brings the ball within his reach.

2. Penalty

A penalty of one run for a wide shall be scored if no runs are made otherwise.

3. Ball Coming to Rest in Front of the Striker

If a ball which the Umpire considers to have been delivered comes to rest in front of the line of the Striker's wicket, "wide" shall not be called. The Striker has a right, without interference from the fielding side, to make one attempt to hit the ball. If the fielding side interferes, the Umpire shall replace the ball where it came to rest and shall order the Fieldsmen to resume the places they occupied in the field before the ball was delivered.

The Umpire shall call and signal "dead ball" as soon as it is clear that the Striker does not intend to hit the ball, or after the Striker has made one successful attempt to hit the ball.

4. Revoking a Call
The Umpire shall revoke the call if the Striker hits a ball which has been called "wide".

5. Ball Not Dead
The ball does not become dead on the call of "wide ball" — see Law 23.4 (The Ball is Not Dead).

6. Runs Resulting from a Wide
All runs which are run or result from a wide ball which is not a no ball shall be scored wide balls, or if no runs are made one [run] shall be scored.

7. Out from a Wide
The Striker shall be out from a wide ball if he breaks Law 35 (Hit Wicket) or Law 39 (Stumped). Either Batsman may be Run Out and shall be out if he breaks Law 33 (Handled the Ball) or Law 37 (Obstructing the Field).

8. Batsman Given Out off a Wide
Should a Batsman be given out off a wide, the penalty for bowling it shall stand unless runs are otherwise made.

Notes
(a) Wide Ball not Counting in Over:
  A wide ball shall not be reckoned as one of the over — see Law 22.3 (No Ball or Wide Ball).

LAW 26 : BYE AND LEG-BYE

1. Byes
If the ball, not having been called "wide" or "no ball" passes the Striker without touching his bat or person, and any runs are obtained, the Umpire shall signal "bye" and the run or runs shall be credited as such to the batting side.

2. Leg-Byes
If the ball, not having been called "wide" or "no ball" is unintentionally deflected by the Striker's dress or person, except a hand holding the bat, and any runs are obtained the Umpire shall signal "leg-bye" and the run or runs so scored shall be credited as such to the batting side.

  Such leg-byes shall only be scored if, in the opinion of the Umpire, the Striker has:
(a) attempted to play the ball with his bat, or
(b) tried to avoid being hit by the ball.

3. Disallowance of Leg-Byes

In the case of a deflection by the Striker's person, other than in 2 (a) and (b) above, the Umpire shall call and signal "dead ball" as soon as one run has been completed or when it is clear that a run is not being attempted or the ball has reached the boundary.

On the call and signal of "dead ball" the Batsmen shall return to their original ends and no runs shall be allowed.

LAW 27 : APPEALS

1. Time of Appeals

The Umpires shall not give a Batsman out unless appealed to by the other side which shall be done prior to the Bowler beginning his run-up or bowling action to deliver the next ball. Under Law 23.1 (g) (The Ball Becomes Dead) the ball is dead on "over" being called; this does not, however, invalidate an appeal made prior to the first ball of the following over provided "time" has not been called. See Law 17.1 (Call of Time).

2. An Appeal "How's That?"

An appeal "How's That?" shall cover all ways of being out.

3. Answering Appeals

The Umpire at the Bowler's wicket shall answer appeals before the other Umpire in all cases except those arising out of Law 35 (Hit Wicket) or Law 39 (Stumped) or Law 38 (Run Out) when this occurs at the Striker's wicket.

When either Umpire has given a Batsman not out, the other Umpire shall, within his jurisdiction, answer the appeal or a further appeal, provided it is made in time in accordance with (1) above (Time of Appeals).

4. Consultation by Umpires

An Umpire may consult with the other Umpire on a point of fact which the latter may have been in a better position to see and shall then give his decision. If, after consultation, there is still doubt remaining the decision shall be in favour of the Batsman.

5. Batsman Leaving His Wicket under a Misapprehension

The Umpires shall intervene if satisfied that a Batsman, not having been given out, has left his wicket under a misapprehension that he has been dismissed.

6. Umpire's Decision

The Umpire's decision is final. He may alter his decision, provided that such alteration is made promptly.

7. Withdrawal of an Appeal

In exceptional circumstances the Captain of the fielding side may seek permission of the Umpire to withdraw an appeal providing (*sic*) the outgoing Batsman has not left the playing area. If this is allowed, the Umpire shall cancel his decision.

LAW 28 : THE WICKET IS DOWN

1. Wicket Down

The wicket is down if:

(a) Either the ball of the Striker's bat or person completely removes either bail from the top of the stumps. A disturbance of a bail, whether temporary or not, shall not constitute a complete removal, but the wicket is down if a bail in falling lodges between two of the stumps.

(b) Any player completely removes with his hand or arm a bail from the top of the stumps, providing (*sic*) that the ball is held in that hand or in the hand of the arm so used.

(c) When both bails are off, a stump is struck out of the ground by the ball, or a player strikes or pulls a stump out of the ground, providing (*sic*) that the ball is held in the hand(s) or in the hand of the arm so used.

2. One Bail Off

If one bail is off, it shall be sufficient for the purpose of putting the wicket down to remove the remaining bail, or to strike or pull any of the three stumps out of the ground in any of the ways stated in (1) above.

3. All the Stumps Out of the Ground

If all the stumps are out of the ground, the fielding side shall be allowed to put back one or more stumps in order to have an opportunity of putting the wicket down.

4. Dispensing with Bails

If owing to the strength of the wind, it has been agreed to dispense with the bails in accordance with Law 8, Note (a) (Dispensing with Bails) the decision as to when the wicket is down is one for the Umpires to decide on the facts before them. In such circumstances and if the Umpires so decide the wicket shall be held to be down even though a stump has not been struck out of the ground.

Notes

(a) Remaking the Wicket:

If the wicket is broken while the ball is in play, it is not the Umpire's duty to remake the wicket until the ball has become dead — See Law 23 (Dead Ball). A member of the fielding side, however, may remake the wicket in such circumstances.

LAW 29 : BATSMAN OUT OF HIS GROUND

1. When Out of His Ground
A Batsman shall be considered to be out of his ground unless some part of his bat in his hand or of his person is grounded behind the line of the popping crease.

LAW 30 : BOWLED

1. Out Bowled
The Striker shall be out bowled if:
(a) His wicket is bowled down, even if the ball first touches his bat or person.
(b) He breaks his wicket by hitting or kicking the ball on to it before completion of a stroke, or as a result of attempting to guard his wicket. See Law 34.1 (Out — Hit the Ball Twice).

Notes
(a) Out Bowled — not LBW (or lbw).
   The Striker is out Bowled if the ball is deflected on to his wicket even though a decision against him would be justified under Law 36 (Leg Before Wicket).

LAW 31 : TIMED OUT

1. Out Timed Out
An incoming Batsman shall be out Timed Out if he wilfully takes more than two minutes to come in — the two minutes being timed from the moment a wicket falls until the new batsman steps on to the field of play.
   If this is not complied with and if the Umpire is satisfied that the delay was wilful and if an appeal is made, the new Batsman shall be given out by the Umpire at the Bowler's end.

2. Time to be Added
The time taken by the Umpires to investigate the cause of the delay shall be added at the normal close of play.

Notes
(a) Entry in Score Book:
   The correct entry in the score book when a Batsman is given out under this Law is "timed out", and the Bowler does not get credit for the wicket.
(b) Batsmen Crossing on the Field of Play:
   It is an essential duty of the Captains to ensure that the in-going Batsman passes the out-going one before the latter leaves the field of play.

LAW 32 : CAUGHT

1. Out Caught

The striker shall be out Caught if the ball touches his bat or if it touches below the wrist, his hand or glove, holding the bat, and is subsequently held by a Fieldsman before it touches the ground.

2. A Fair Catch

A catch shall be considered to have been fairly made if:

(a) The Fieldsman is within the field of play throughout the act of making the catch.

  (i) The act of making the catch shall start from the time when the Fieldsman first handles the ball and shall end when he both retains complete control over the further disposal of the ball and remains within the field of play.

  (ii) In order to be within the field of play, the Fieldsman may not touch or ground any part of his person on or over a boundary line. When the boundary is marked by a fence or board the Fieldsman may not ground any part of his person over the boundary fence or board, but may touch or lean over the boundary fence or board in completing the catch.

(b) The ball is hugged to the body of the catcher or accidentally lodges in his dress or, in the case of the Wicket-Keeper, in his pads. However, a Striker may not be caught if a ball lodges in a protective helmet worn by a Fieldsman, in which case the Umpire shall call and signal "dead ball". See Law 23 (Dead Ball).

(c) The ball does not touch the ground even though a hand holding it does so in effecting the catch.

(d) A Fieldsman catches the ball, after it has been lawfully played a second time by the Striker, but only if the ball has not touched the ground since being first struck.

(e) A Fieldsman catches the ball after it has touched an Umpire, another Fieldsman or the other Batsman. However a Striker may not be caught if a ball has touched a protective helmet worn by a Fieldsman.

(f) The ball is caught off an obstruction within the boundary provided it has not previously been agreed to regard the obstruction as a boundary.

3. Scoring of Runs

If a Striker is caught, no runs shall be scored.

Notes

(a) Scoring from an Attempted Catch:
   When a Fieldsman carrying the ball touches or grounds any part of his person on or over a boundary marked by a line, 6 runs shall be scored.

(b) Ball Still in Play:
   If a Fieldsman releases the ball before he crosses the boundary, the ball will be considered

to be still in play and it may be caught by another Fieldsman. However, if the original
Fieldsman returns to the field of play and handles the ball, a catch may not be made.

LAW 33 : HANDLED THE BALL

1. Out Handled the Ball
Either Batsman on appeal shall be out Handled the Ball if he wilfully touches the ball
while in play with the hand not holding the bat unless he does so with the consent
of the opposite side.

Notes
(a) Entry in Score Book:
   The correct entry in the score book when a Batsman is given out under this Law is "handled
   the ball", and the Bowler does not get credit for the wicket.

LAW 34 : HIT THE BALL TWICE

1. Out Hit the Ball Twice
The Striker, on appeal, shall be out Hit the Ball Twice if, after the ball is struck or
is stopped by any part of his person, he wilfully strikes it again with his bat or person
except for the sole purpose of guarding his wicket : this he may do with his bat or any
part of his person other than his hands, but see Law 37.2 (Obstructing a Ball from
Being Caught).
   For the purpose of this Law, a hand holding the bat shall be regarded as part of the bat.

2. Returning the Ball to a Fieldsman
The Striker, on appeal, shall be out under this Law, if, without the consent of the
opposite side, he uses his bat or person to return the ball to any of the fielding side.

3. Runs from Ball Lawfully Struck Twice
No runs except those which result from an overthrow or penalty, see Law 41 (The
Fieldsman), shall be scored from a ball lawfully struck twice.

Notes
(a) Entry in Score Book:
   The correct entry in the score book when the Striker is given out under this Law is "hit
   the ball twice", and the Bowler does not get credit for the wicket.
(b) Runs Credited to the Batsman:
   Any runs awarded under (3) above as a result of an overthrow or penalty shall be credited
   to the Striker, provided the ball in the first instance has touched the bat, or, if otherwise
   as extras.

LAW 35 : HIT WICKET

1. Out Hit Wicket

The Striker shall be out Hit Wicket if, while the ball is in play:

(a) His wicket is broken with any part of his person, dress, or equipment as a result of any action taken by him in preparing to receive or in receiving a delivery, or in setting off for his first run, immediately after playing, or playing at, the ball.

(b) He hits down his wicket whilst lawfully making a second stroke for the purpose of guarding his wicket within the provisions of Law 34.1 (Out Hit the Ball Twice).

Notes

(a) Not Out Hit Wicket:

A Batsman is not out under this Law should his wicket be broken in any of the ways referred to in 1 (a) above if:

　(i) *It occurs while he is in the act of running, other than in setting off for his first run immediately after playing at the ball, or while he is avoiding being run out or stumped.*

　(ii) *The Bowler after starting his run-up or bowling action does not deliver the ball; in which case the Umpire shall immediately call and signal "dead ball".*

　(iii) *It occurs whilst he is avoiding a throw-in at any time.*

LAW 36 : LEG BEFORE WICKET (LBW)

1. Out LBW

The Striker shall be out LBW in the circumstances set out below:

(a) Striker Attempting to Play the Ball:

The Striker shall be out LBW if he first intercepts with any part of his person, dress or equipment a fair ball which would have hit the wicket and which has not previously touched his bat or a hand holding the bat, provided that:

　(i) the ball pitched, in a straight line between wicket and wicket or on the off side of the Striker's wicket, or in the case of a ball intercepted full pitch would have pitched in a straight line between wicket and wicket, and

　(ii) the point of impact is in a straight line between wicket and wicket, even if above the level of the bails.

(b) Striker Making No Attempt to Play the Ball:

The Striker shall be out LBW even if the ball is intercepted outside the line of the off-stump, if, in the opinion of the Umpire, he has made no genuine attempt to play the ball with his bat, but has intercepted the ball with some part of his person and if the circumstances set out in (a) above apply.

LAW 37 : OBSTRUCTING THE FIELD

1. Wilful Obstruction
Either Batsman, on appeal, shall be out Obstructing the Field if he wilfully obstructs the opposite side by word or action.

2. Obstructing a Ball from being Caught
The Striker, on appeal, shall be out should wilful obstruction by either Batsman prevent a catch being made.

This shall apply even though the Striker causes the obstruction in lawfully guarding his wicket under the provisions of Law 34. See Law 34.1 (Out Hit the Ball Twice).

Notes
(a) Accidental Obstruction:
   The Umpires must decide whether the obstruction was wilful or not. The accidental interception of a throw-in by a Batsman while running does not break this Law.
(b) Entry in Score Book:
   The correct entry in the score book when a Batsman is given out under this Law is "obstructing the field", and the bowler does not get credit for the wicket.

LAW 38 : RUN OUT

1. Out Run Out
Either Batsman shall be out Run Out if in running or at any time while the ball is in play — except in the circumstances described in Law 39 (Stumped) — he is out of his ground and his wicket is put down by the opposite side. If, however, a Batsman in running makes good his ground he shall not be out Run Out, if he subsequently leaves his ground, in order to avoid injury, and the wicket is put down.

2. "No Ball" Called
If a no ball has been called, the Striker shall not be given Run Out unless he attempts to run.

3. Which Batsman Is Out
If the Batsmen have crossed in running, he who runs for the wicket which is put down shall be out; if they have not crossed, he who has left the wicket which is put down shall be out. If a Batsman remains in his ground or returns to his ground and the other Batsman joins him there, the latter shall be out if his wicket is put down.

4. Scoring of Runs
If a Batsman is run out, only that run which is being attempted shall not be scored.

If however an injured Striker himself is run out, no runs shall be scored. See Law 2.7 (Transgression of the Laws by an Injured Batsman or Runner).

Notes

(a) Ball Played on to Opposite Wicket:
   If the ball is played on to the opposite wicket neither Batsman is liable to be Run Out unless the ball has been touched by a Fieldsman before the wicket is broken.

(b) Entry in Score Book:
   The correct entry in the score book when the Striker is given out under this Law is "run out", and the Bowler does not get credit for the wicket.

LAW 39 : STUMPED

1. Out Stumped
The Striker shall be out Stumped if, in receiving a ball, not being a no ball, he is out of his ground otherwise than in attempting a run and the wicket is put down by the Wicket-Keeper without the intervention of another Fieldsman.

2. Action by the Wicket-Keeper
The Wicket-Keeper may take the ball in front of the wicket in an attempt to Stump the Striker only if the ball has touched the bat or person of the Striker.

Notes

(a) Ball Rebounding from Wicket-Keeper's Person:
   The Striker may be out Stumped if in the circumstances stated in (1) above, the wicket is broken by a ball rebounding from the Wicket-Keeper's person or equipment or is kicked or thrown by the Wicket-Keeper on to the wicket.

LAW 40 : THE WICKET-KEEPER

1. Position of Wicket-Keeper
The Wicket-Keeper shall remain wholly behind the wicket until a ball delivered by the Bowler touches the bat or person of the Striker, or passes the wicket, or until the Striker attempts a run.

In the event of the Wicket-Keeper contravening this Law, the Umpire at the Striker's end shall call and signal "no ball" at the instant of delivery or as soon as possible thereafter.

2. Restriction on Actions of the Wicket-Keeper
If the Wicket-Keeper interferes with the Striker's right to play the ball and to guard his wicket, the Striker shall not be out, except under Laws 33 (Handled the Ball), 34 (Hit the Ball Twice), 37 (Obstructing the Field) and 38 (Run Out).

3. Interference with the Wicket-Keeper by the Striker
If in the legitimate defence of his wicket, the Striker interferes with the Wicket-Keeper, he shall not be out, except as provided for in Law 37.2 (Obstructing a Ball from Being Caught).

LAW 41 : THE FIELDSMAN

1. Fielding the Ball
The Fieldsman may stop the ball with any part of his person, but if he wilfully stops it otherwise, 5 runs shall be added to the run or runs already scored; if no run has been scored 5 penalty runs shall be awarded. The run in progress shall count provided that the Batsmen have crossed at the instant of the act. If the ball has been struck, the penalty shall be added to the score of the Striker, but otherwise to the score of byes, leg-byes, no balls or wides as the case may be.

2. Limitation of On-Side Fieldsmen
The number of on-side Fieldsmen behind the popping crease at the instant of the Bowler's delivery shall not exceed two. In the event of infringement by the fielding side the Umpire at the Striker's end shall call and signal "no ball" at the instant of delivery or as soon as possible thereafter.

3. Position of Fieldsmen
Whilst the ball is in play and until the ball has made contact with the bat or the Striker's person or has passed his bat, no Fieldsman, other than the Bowler, may stand on or have any part of his person extended over the pitch (measuring 22 yards /20.12 m x 10 ft/3.05 m). In the event of a Fieldsman contravening this Law, the Umpire at the bowler's end shall call and signal "no ball" at the instant of delivery or as soon as possible thereafter. See Law 40.1 (Position of Wicket-Keeper).

4. Fieldsmen's Protective Helmets
Protective helmets, when not in use by members of the fielding side, shall only be placed, if above the surface, on the ground behind the Wicket-Keeper. In the event of the ball, when in play, striking a helmet whilst in this position, five penalty runs shall be awarded, as laid down in Law 41.1 and Note (a).

Notes
(a) Batsmen Changing Ends:
The 5 runs referred to in (1) above are a penalty and the Batsmen do not change ends solely by reason of this penalty.

LAW 42 : UNFAIR PLAY

1. Responsibility of Captains
The Captains are responsible at all times for ensuring that play is conducted within the spirit of the game as well as within the Laws.

2. Responsibility of Umpires
The Umpires are the sole judges of fair and unfair play.

3. Intervention by the Umpires
The Umpires shall intervene without appeal by calling and signalling "dead ball" in the case of unfair play, but should not otherwise interfere with the progress of the game except as required to do so by the Laws.

4. Lifting the Seam
A Player shall not lift the seam of the ball for any reason. Should this be done, the Umpires shall change the ball for one of similar conditions to that in use prior to the contravention. See Note (a) [to this section].

5. Changing the Condition of the Ball
Any member of the fielding side may polish the ball provided that such polishing wastes no time and that no artificial substance is used. No one shall rub the ball on the ground or use any artificial substance or take any other action to alter the condition of the ball. In the event of a contravention of this Law, the Umpires, after consultation, shall change the ball for one of similar conditions to that in use prior to the contravention.

This Law does not prevent a member of the fielding side from drying a wet ball, or removing mud from the ball. See Note (b) [to this section].

6. Incommoding the Striker
An Umpire is justified in intervening under this Law and shall call and signal "dead ball" if, in his opinion, any Player of the fielding side incommodes the Striker by any noise or action while he is receiving a ball.

7. Obstruction of a Batsman in Running
It shall be considered unfair if any Fieldsman wilfully obstructs a Batsman in running. In these circumstances the Umpire shall call and signal "dead ball" and allow any completed runs and the run in progress or alternatively any boundary scored.

8. The Bowling of Fast Short Pitched Balls
The bowling of fast short pitched balls is unfair if, in the opinion of the Umpire at the Bowler's end, it constitutes an attempt to intimidate the Striker. See Note (d) [to this section].

Umpires shall consider intimidation to be the deliberate bowling of fast short pitched balls which by their length, height and direction are intended or likely to inflict physical injury on the Striker. The relative skill of the Striker shall also be taken into consideration.

In the event of such unfair bowling, the Umpire at the Bowler's end shall adopt the following procedure:-

(a) In the first instance the Umpire shall call and signal "no ball", caution the Bowler and inform the other Umpire, the Captain of the fielding side and the Batsmen of what has occurred.

(b) If this caution is ineffective, he shall repeat the above procedure and indicate to the Bowler that this is a final warning.

(c) Both the above caution and final warning shall continue to apply even though the Bowler may later change ends.

(d) Should the above warnings prove ineffective the Umpire at the Bowler's end shall:

  (i) At the first repetition call and signal "no ball" and when the ball is dead direct the Captain to take the Bowler off forthwith and to complete the over with another Bowler, provided that the Bowler does not bowl two overs of part thereof consecutively. See Law 22.7 (Bowler Incapacitated or Suspended during an Over).

  (ii) Not allow the Bowler, thus taken off, to bowl again in the same innings.

  (iii) Report the occurrence to the Captain of the batting side as soon as the Players leave the field for an interval.

  (iv) Report the occurrence to the Executive of the fielding side and to any governing body responsible for the match who shall take any further action which is considered to be appropriate against the Bowler concerned.

9. The Bowling of Fast High Full Pitches

The bowling of fast high full pitches is unfair. See Note (e) [to this section]. In the event of such unfair bowling the Umpire at the bowler's end shall adopt the procedures of caution, final warning, action against the Bowler and reporting as set out in (8) above.

10. Time Wasting

Any form of time wasting is unfair.

(a) In the event of the Captain of the fielding side wasting time or allowing any member of his side to waste time, the Umpire at the Bowler's end shall adopt the following procedure:

  (i) In the first instance he shall caution the Captain of the fielding side and inform the other Umpire of what has occurred.

  (ii) If this caution is ineffective he shall repeat the above procedure and indicate to the Captain that this is a final warning.

    (iii) The Umpire shall report the occurrence to the Captain of the batting side as soon as the Players leave the field for an interval.

    (iv) Should the above procedure prove ineffective the Umpire shall report the occurrence to the Executive of the fielding side and to any governing body responsible for that match who shall take appropriate action against the Captain and the Players concerned.

(b) In the event of a Bowler taking unnecessarily long to bowl an over the Umpire at the Bowler's end shall adopt the procedures, other than the calling of "no ball", of caution, final warning, action against the Bowler and reporting.

(c) In the event of a Batsman wasting time [see Note [f] to this section] other than in the manner described in Law 31 (Timed Out), the Umpire at the Bowler's end shall adopt the following procedure:

    (i) In the first instance he shall caution the Batsman and inform the other Umpire at once, and the Captain of the batting side, as soon as the players leave the field for an interval, of what has occurred.

    (ii) If this proves ineffective, he shall repeat the caution, indicate to the Batsman that this is a final warning and inform the other Umpire.

    (iii) The Umpire shall report the occurrence to both Captains as soon as the Players leave the field for an interval.

    (iv) Should the above procedure prove ineffective, the Umpire shall report the occurrence to the Executive of the batting side and to any governing body responsible for that match who shall take appropriate action against the player concerned.

11. Players Damaging the Pitch

The Umpires shall intervene and prevent Players from causing damage to the pitch which may assist the Bowlers of either side. See Note (c) [to this section].

(a) In the event of any member of the fielding side damaging the pitch the Umpire shall follow the procedure of caution, final warning and reporting as set out in 10 (a) above.

(b) In the event of a Bowler contravening this Law by running down the pitch after delivering the ball, the Umpire at the Bowler's end shall first caution the Bowler. If this caution is ineffective, the Umpire shall adopt the procedure, other than the calling of "no ball", of final warning, action against the Bowler and reporting.

(c) In the event of a Batsman damaging the pitch the Umpire at the Bowler's end shall follow the procedures of caution, final warning and reporting as set out in 10 (c) above.

12. Batsman Unfairly Stealing a Run

Any attempt by the Batsman to steal a run during the Bowler's run-up is unfair. Unless the Bowler attempts to run out either Batsman — see Law 24.4 (Bowler Throwing at

Striker's Wicket before Delivery) and Law 24.5 (Bowler Attempting to Run Out Non-Striker before Delivery) — the Umpire shall call and signal "dead ball" as soon as the Batsmen cross in any such attempt to run. The Batsmen shall then return to their original wickets.

13. Players' Conduct

In the event of a player failing to comply with the instructions of an Umpire, criticising his decisions by word or action, or showing dissent, or generally behaving in a manner which might bring the game into disrepute, the Umpire concerned shall, in the first place, report the matter to the other Umpire and to the Player's Captain requesting the latter to take action. If this proves ineffective, the Umpire shall report the incident as soon as possible to the Executive of the Player's team and to any Governing Body responsible for the match, who shall take any further action which is considered appropriate against the Player or Players concerned.

Note

(a) The Condition of the Ball:
   Umpires shall make frequent and irregular inspections of the condition of the ball.

(b) Drying of a Wet Ball:
   A wet ball may be dried on a towel or with sawdust.

(c) Danger Area:
   The danger area on the pitch, which must be protected from damage by a Bowler, shall be regarded by the Umpires as the area contained by an imaginary line 4 ft/1.22 m from the popping crease, and parallel to it, and within two imaginary and parallel lines drawn down the pitch from points on that line 1 ft/30.48 cm on either side of the middle stump.

(d) Fast Short Pitched Balls:
   As a guide, a fast short pitched ball is one which pitches short and passes, or would have passed, above the shoulder height of the Striker standing in a normal batting stance at the crease.

(e) The Bowling of Fast Full Pitches:
   The Bowling of one fast, high full pitch shall be considered to be unfair if, in the opinion of the Umpire, it is deliberate, bowled at the Striker, and if it passes or would have passed above the shoulder height of the Striker when standing in a normal batting stance at the crease.

(f) Time Wasting by Batsmen:
   Other than in exceptional circumstances, the Batsman should always be ready to take strike when the Bowler is ready to start his run-up.

Index